THE BASTILLE
OF IRELAND

THE BASTILLE OF IRELAND

KILMAINHAM GAOL:
FROM RUIN TO RESTORATION

RORY O'DWYER

The History Press Ireland

First published 2010

The History Press Ireland
119 Lower Baggot Street
Dublin 2
Ireland
www.thehistorypress.ie

British Library Cataloguing in Publication Data.
A catalogue record for this book is available from the British Library.

ISBN 978 1 84588 973 9

Typesetting and origination by The History Press
Printed in Great Britain
Manufacturing managed by Jellyfish Print Solutions Ltd

CONTENTS

ACKNOWLEDGEMENTS

Many individuals contributed and helped directly or indirectly in the research and preparation of this work. As a former guide in Kilmainham Jail I am enormously indebted to so many other members of staff at Kilmainham both past and present, including Niall Bergin, Mícheál Ó Doibhilín, Liz Gillis, Niamh O'Sullivan, Pat Cooke, Tim Carey, Conor Masterson, Ann-Marie Ryan, Brian Crowley, Helen Murphy, Gavan Woods, Phyl Mason, Cara Ronan, Sarah Delaney and Catherine O'Connor. This list could continue to a very considerable length; so many have been both brilliant company and an inspiration to me at various times while working in Kilmainham. I am very grateful for the opportunity to avail of so much material from the museum archives. I also wish to express my gratitude to staff at the National Archives of Ireland, the National Library of Ireland, the UCC Library and the Dublin City Library. Special thanks to Margot and Aoibhe for their support.

INTRODUCTION

Kilmainham Jail,[1] now a national monument, is a unique resource in the study of modern Irish history. At intervals in this country's difficult and turbulent passage from the 1790s to the 1920s, the jail was to hold men and women who played leading roles in shaping the island on which we live. Among the most renowned prisoners held in Kilmainham were Robert Emmet, Jeremiah O'Donovan Rossa, Charles Stuart Parnell and, most famously, the 1916 leaders, prior to their execution within the jail. Indeed, leading figures in every rebellion directed against British rule since 1798 are associated with the jail.[2] Éamon de Valera, by coincidence the very last prisoner held in the jail, was later Taoiseach and President of Ireland. However, Kilmainham Jail also contained bitter Civil War memories, as four young Republicans were executed in the prison in 1922 (the first executions carried out by the Irish Free State army during the Civil War).[3] Perhaps this helps to explain why the building was allowed to fall into ruin after its closure in 1924 – a legacy too difficult to remember.

In 1932, however, with the coming to power of a new government with many cabinet ministers and party members who had been prisoners in Kilmainham during the Civil War,[4] it is understandable that there might have been an interest in establishing the jail as a nationalist monument. Indeed, with its apparently obvious associations with British and Free State 'misrule', it may have seemed a very interesting idea to develop the site's potential. The very notion of restoring the jail, with its easily emphasised associations of sacrifice and patriotism, could fit very appropriately (on a surface level at least) with the predominant nationalist ethos of the time.

Kilmainham Jail certainly had the potential to become a celebrated 'Bastille of Ireland'. However, for a number of reasons, that early Fianna Fáil administration did not exploit the potential of the site. In fact, although it was often given consideration by various governments over a period of nearly thirty years, it was not until 1960 that restoration work on the jail actually began. The task was eventually carried out, not by the state but by a voluntary group which became known as the Kilmainham Jail Restoration Society.

In many respects, the story of the jail since 1924 has proved just as absorbing as its revolutionary past. Contained within the jail museum archives today are documents relating to the restoration, such as minutes of the early meetings of the Trustees, letters to government ministers, and other material outlining the ideals and determination of the original restoration committee. The archives also include records of various commemorations and other events held in the jail since 1960. It is worth stressing the central role played by the jail in 1966 during the elaborate fiftieth anniversary commemorations of the 1916 Rising, by which time the most important restoration work had been completed. The commemoration of the Rising since the Jubilee year reveals much about evolving official and popular attitudes to Irish history and identity, and as Kilmainham Jail is one of the most iconic sites associated with the Rising, commemorative events held in the jail reveal much about public and government feelings through time.

Above left: United Irishman Henry Joy McCracken, imprisoned in Kilmainham October 1796–December 1797. He was hanged in Belfast in July 1798. (Courtesy of Kilmainham Jail Museum Archives.)

Above right: The Wicklow rebel Michael Dwyer, imprisoned in Kilmainham December 1803–July 1805. He was then transported to New South Wales, where he died in 1825.

Above left: Thomas Francis Meagher (second from left) and William Smith O'Brien (seated, third from left) in Kilmainham Jail. They were transported to Van Diemen's Land in 1849.

Above right: Ernie O'Malley, twice a prisoner in Kilmainham (1920/21 and 1923). He was one of the few to have escaped from the jail.

In order to describe the various events that have taken place in Kilmainham since 1960 (which include historical exhibitions, plays, film-making, concerts, etc.) I refer to various newspapers, periodicals and other such sources of the times. This book has also necessitated research work in the National Archives, in particular to study the early plans and considerations for the restoration of the prison from the 1930s onwards. When the jail was taken over by the Office of Public Works in 1986, the changeover marked the end of the Kilmainham Jail Restoration Society and this book concludes with a summary of notable events from 1986 to the present day in order to demonstrate how the enthusiasm and spirit of the early voluntary workers involved in the restoration project has lived on, but also how the jail, as a modern museum, has adapted to maintain an abiding relevance in contemporary cultural life.

The essential aim here is to document an untold story of great ambition and purpose, though one often marked by frustration and procrastination; a project which would eventually ensure that Kilmainham Jail would provide a unique and highly valuable resource in a study of modern Irish history.

1

FALLING INTO RUIN

Following the removal of the last Republican prisoners in the early months of 1924, Kilmainham Jail was never again used as a place of confinement. The prison was evacuated by the Irish Free State army in March of that year, when care of the jail reverted to the General Prisons Board of Ireland.[5] Having no need for the prison at the time, the Prisons Board carried out no maintenance whatsoever on the building over the following years and the jail began to fall into disrepair. The very first proposal for use of the jail for purposes other than a prison was to come from a most unlikely source. A German engineering company, *Siemens Schukert*, contractors for the Shannon Hydro-Electric Scheme, approached the Prisons Board in 1926 requesting the use of the prison compound as a storage depot for masts and other weighty material. The location of the jail was considered particularly suitable, as the contractors were planning to build a transformer station in Inchicore and the jail was also in close proximity to Kingsbridge (Heuston) Station, where a special rail truck had been designed to transport materials from Dublin to Limerick and on to Ardnacrusha, on the Shannon. The contractors were especially interested in using the yards on the north-west side of the prison. These yards happened to be the old stonebreaker's yard, where the 1916 leaders were executed, and an adjacent yard where four republicans were executed during the Civil War.

Although the proposal could be considered very insensitive, the Prisons Board actually agreed to the request. The offer of the contractors to demolish the west wing of the jail (the older section) for improved storage space appealed to the board, who wished to avoid the expense of demolishing it themselves. If Kilmainham Jail was ever to be used again as a prison, the board had already decided that only the Victorian east wing would be suitable. Although the proposed demolition did not take place, the contractors did avail of the prison building from early 1927. Rooms at the front of the building were occupied by a number of German engineers and the jail was used as a store.[6] This arrangement may have continued until the Shannon scheme was completed in 1929.

A Statutory Order closing the premises was made by the Minister of Justice on 1 August 1929, and in accordance with the General Prisons (Ireland) Act 1877, Kilmainham Jail was automatically transferred to Dublin County Council on the expiration of one year from that date.[7] As a government memorandum later summarised, 'the legal position therefore was that the State's interest in Kilmainham Jail had lapsed and nothing under existing statutes could revive it'.[8]

It was never very likely that the Cumann na nGaedheal government would express an interest in preserving the jail as any sort of national shrine. Given the aforementioned bitter Civil War memories connected with the jail, there was also a general pattern beginning to emerge from 1923 – a reluctance, or at least a pronounced lack of enthusiasm to celebrate even that *fons et origo* of the independent Irish state, the 1916 Rising. An example of this reluctance became evident in October 1923, when Clement Shorter, whose recently deceased wife was the nationalist poet and sculptor Nora Sigerson, offered to contribute £1,000 from his wife's estate to enable her sculpture commemorating the 1916 leaders to be fashioned in Carrera marble, set on a pedestal of Irish limestone, and erected in Glasnevin Cemetery.[9] W.T. Cosgrave, however, expressed concern that the proposal would make it 'look as if we wanted to have one last slap at the British'.[10] Nevertheless, in December 1923, the Executive Council of the Irish Free State eventually decided to approve the proposal. This was, however, followed by an extremely prolonged sequence of setbacks and quandaries. Eventually, in May 1927, the memorial was completed in Glasnevin but qualified with 'a characteristic decision to avoid any formal ceremony of unveiling and hence reduce the risk of an unseemly public squabble over the Easter inheritance'.[11]

Exterior of the jail in 1929.

The east wing of the jail (sometimes referred to as the main compound or main hall in the restoration years) was completed in 1861.

Instead of any public procession to commemorate the Rising, the Executive Council decided in 1924 on a closed ceremony in Arbour Hill Detention Barracks, where the executed leaders of the Rising are buried. This was the first official 1916 commemoration ceremony. It was, however, considerably marred by a very poor attendance. Although twenty-five relatives of the deceased men were invited to attend, only one, the wife of Michael Mallin, actually attended the ceremony.[17] All of the others chose not to attend due to their objections to the Free State authority.

Also in 1924, the first major public procession to commemorate 1916 took place in the shape of a march from the General Post Office to Glasnevin Cemetery for the laying of wreaths on the republican plot – where most of those who were killed on the rebel side (other than those executed in Kilmainham Jail) are buried. The event was organised by republicans, and the Free State government took no part in it. Thousands of people were reported to have gathered at the cemetery. Similar demonstrations took place in other parts of the country. This pattern of large popular processions organised by republicans and discreet, somewhat awkward, commemoration by the state was to continue throughout Cumann na nGaedheal's tenure in office.

All the while, Kilmainham Jail was falling into a very poor condition. In 1931, an *Irish Independent* reporter noted the deterioration of the building in an article that attracted some interest:

> In many respects it [Kilmainham Jail] is a wreck. Most of the windows have been smashed, and many fittings removed, including fireplaces, but by whom nobody appears to know. Most astounding of all was the information given on good authority to an *Irish Independent* representative that some of the beams of the execution chamber were sawn away [and] are now used in a Dublin tennis court. What were once used for hanging Irishmen are now being used for hanging tennis nets. Other things, not so 'convertable', have not been removed, but their value in most cases has much depreciated.[13]

Above: The older west wing, most of which dates to the 1790s.

Opposite: Plan of the jail. The east wing is to the left, the west wing to the right.

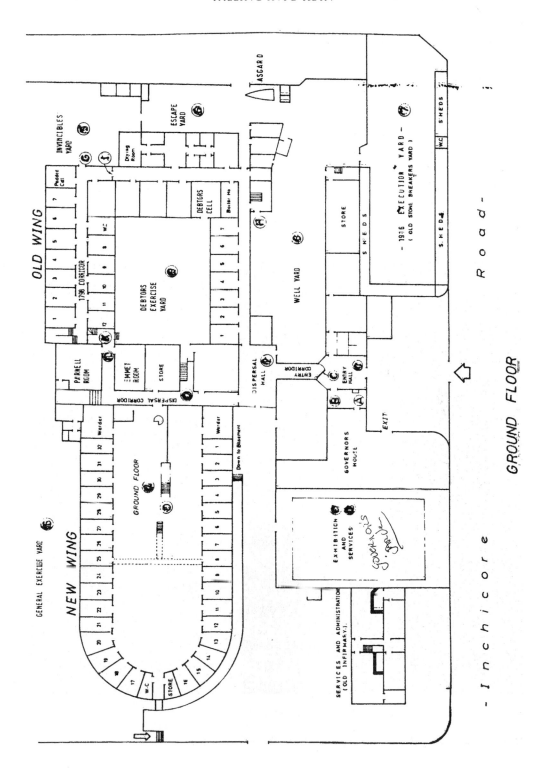

The *Independent* received a number of letters to the editor regarding the article, most particularly to express dismay and outrage at the findings of the reporter. At a meeting of Dublin County Council, a resolution was introduced that the Minister for Justice, James Fitzgerald Kenney (whose department had until recently been responsible for the jail), should be charged with criminal negligence.

Dublin County Council soon came under pressure over its recent acquisition. Letters were immediately received from the National Graves Association (NGA) enquiring as to the council's intentions with the property.[13] The NGA had been formed in 1926 with the central objectives of restoring, where necessary, and maintaining in a fitting manner the graves and memorials of Ireland's patriot dead of every generation, compiling a record of such graves and memorials, and commemorating all those who died in the cause of Irish freedom.[14] They had a understandable interest in having a permanent commemoration to some of those executed in Kilmainham Jail.[15]

2

PROPOSALS CONSIDERED

The attempts by the NGA to secure a memorial at Kilmainham were always spearheaded by Seán Fitzpatrick, the honorary secretary of the association. Fitzpatrick, who worked as a road sweeper for Dublin Corporation in the Kilmainham area, had used his exceptional local knowledge and awareness to assist in organising the renowned 1921 escape of three Volunteers (Ernie O'Malley, Frank Teeling and Simon Donnelly) from the jail. Living locally, he had always maintained a fascination with the prison. Fitzpatrick now repeatedly wrote to the council outlining his vision of the jail as a national monument.[16] He urged the council to consider opening the jail for visitors during the Eucharistic Congress in the summer of 1932, to highlight Irish patriotic endeavour to both Irish people and to the many foreign visitors.[17] His suggestion was, however, not approved by the council.

While expressing sympathy for the cause of the NGA, the County Council claimed that it did not have the necessary funding to carry out such work.[18] On 7 December 1932, Fitzpatrick, wrote to the Minister for Local Government, Seán T. O'Kelly (a member of the Fianna Fáil minority government elected earlier that year and a prisoner in Kilmainham during the Civil War), requesting that he would 'receive a deputation from our body to discuss the question of permanently marking the place where the men of 1916 and four of the 1922 men were shot, also the enclosing of the place of burial of the men hanged in 1883 [The Invincibles] '.[19]

One week later, O'Kelly wrote to Éamon de Valera, President of the Executive Council, on the matter. He expressed a conviction that the jail could be considered a national monument, within the definition in Section 2, National Monument Act, 1930.[20] Although remarking that the County Council therefore had a duty of care to the jail, he asserted that 'it would not be appropriate or satisfactory that an assumption would arise that the matter could be left to the council for attention'. O'Kelly concluded by advising:

Perhaps the best course will be that you pass this correspondence to the Minister of Finance, who through the Commissioners of Public Works can advise. I think the government should assume sole responsibility and someone on the government's behalf should see the Secretary of the County Council so that there may be as little delay as possible.[21]

De Valera appears to have approved of the proposal, and the matter was duly passed on to the Commissioners of Public Works (CPW), who tentatively began to approach the County Council with a view to ascertaining their terms. The first of a number of surveys and estimates on the jail were carried out by CPW officials. In consultation with the National Museum, the CPW began to seriously consider developing the jail as a museum.

Early proposals by the CPW, however, found opposition from the Minister for Education, Tomás Derrig, who expressed the view that the buildings were generally unsuitable for conversion to museum purposes.[22] As an alternative, the Department put forward a suggestion by the Director of the National Museum, Adolf Mahr, that, following the example of nationalist Spain, where the former republican prison in Madrid was preserved as a place of remembrance, the galleries and cells should be retained in their existing state and that memorial tablets should be provided to recall the history of the liberation movements.[23] In other words, the jail would be more a shrine than a museum – there would be no need for any exhibits.

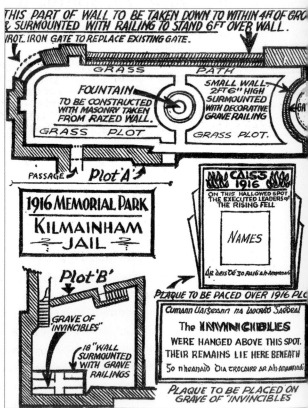

Above left: Seán Fitzpatrick, honorary secretary of the National Graves Association.

Above right: Fitzpatrick's plans for the jail.

KILMAINHAM JAIL

PROPOSED NATIONAL BOXING STADIUM

The Irish Amateur Boxing Association has made a request to the Dublin Co. Council to be given a portion of the now derelict Kilmainham Jail for conversion into a National Boxing Stadium.

It is understood that the I.A.B.A. have plans whereby a first-class public hall, with accommodation for 3,000 people, can be constructed by a modification of the present structure. The plans cater for the most modern lighting, heating, and seating accommodation.

In addition, it is the intention to preserve, as a reminder to future generations of young Irishmen, certain portions of he building intimately connected with leading Irishmen, as well as to commemorate the names of those so associated.

Boxing stadium proposal for the jail.

This suggestion possibly reflected the National Museum's concerns that their most popular collections, those illustrating the National Risings (including 1916), would be removed from Kildare Street. The Director, Adolf Mahr, stressed that the jail premises was unsatisfactory for museum purposes, both because of its location and the great expense necessary to convert the jail adequately for such purposes.[24] Mahr knew the mentality in the Department of Finance and his emphasis on expenditure probably helped ensure the temporary shelving of the project.

As government and CPW officials procrastinated, Seán Fitzpatrick of the NGA continued to exert pressure for action on Kilmainham. Due to his influence, the matter was raised in the Dáil on 20 February 1936 by the leader of the Labour Party, William Norton, who asked whether or not the government was indeed going to declare the jail a national monument. The Tánaiste, Seán MacEntee, replied that the issue was still under consideration.[25] The matter was also debated to some extent in the press;[26] an editorial in the *Wicklow People* newspaper offered the view that the place should be 'pulled down and its site made a playground for children, after suitably marking and commemorating the graves of the executed there'.[27]

At a meeting of Dublin County Council the Chairman of the Council, P. Belton TD, seemed to dismiss a resolution that the jail be handed over to the government for a national monument by stating his view 'that the jail should be blown to atoms. It was not a place where Irishmen should weep and it should not be made a kind of Wailing Wall of Jerusalem.' He looked on it as an eyesore and a place where Irishmen had been humiliated and persecuted. Another member of the council, R. Blake was also critical of the resolution, 'Why should we hand it over to the government? The Union Jack might soon hang over it if you gave it to that bunch. I would give it over to the IRA themselves.'[28]

However, the government's interest in doing something with Kilmainham did not abate at this time, and at a meeting of the Executive Council on 4 December 1936, it was finally decided that the jail premises would definitely be acquired by the State from the County Council and that the main building[29] would be preserved and the remaining buildings demolished, the site thus obtained being laid out as a public park.[30] Although the jail was indeed acquired by the State soon afterwards, no progress at all was made on developing the site, which continued to decay.[31]

With Seán Fitzpatrick continuing to exert pressure on the government, the media became more interested in the issue. On 14 March 1938, *The Irish Press* featured a prominent article with the title: 'Shall Kilmainham Fall?':

> Shall we rend Kilmainham Jail stone from stone, as did the French with their Bastille, led by the way by a man of Irish blood – or shall we maintain it as a memorial to those who, generation after generation, suffered there for Ireland?[32]

The article went on to elaborate on Fitzpatrick's argument and published his plans for the treatment of the 1916 plot and the 'Invincibles' plot, in the form of a small memorial park. The same article also reported on one of the very occasional visits to the jail permitted to private bodies, the previous Saturday, in order to further the argument to restore the jail:

> That the matter is of great public interest was evidenced on Saturday when at the invitation of the Executive of Old Cumann na mBan, crowds of members and their friends visited the jail and spent the afternoon in visiting theirs or their old friends' old cells, or in increasing their knowledge of the place as a whole.[33]

3

SEÁN HEUSTON MEMORIAL COMMITTEE

Also present on the day were members of the Seán Heuston Memorial Committee, engaged in preparations for the opening of the jail to the public eight days later.[34] The committee had made careful preparations for 'the correct information of visitors and were engaged in instructing the stewards and making out placards to indicate the particularly outstanding incidents'.[35]

With the media interest and a very well-organised publicity campaign by the Seán Heuston Memorial Committee, the open day was extremely successful from a fundraising perspective. Massive crowds turned up at Kilmainham, with busloads coming from Belfast and elsewhere to see the jail. As an *Irish Press* reporter commented, 'Irish history was retraced at Kilmainham yesterday when thousands of people availed themselves of the first public pilgrimage to the prison and visited places sacred to the Irish Race.'[36] An *Irish Times* reporter provided a more level-headed commentary:

> From mid-day to 6p.m. there was a constant stream of people, and the queue, which waited outside for admission stretched at times to about a quarter of a mile. Over a hundred stewards were on duty to act as guides to the various places of interest, and there was also a large detachment of Civic Guards and members of the St John Ambulance Brigade. Most of the guides obviously had a keen interest in their work. They have studied the history of the prison, and many had vivid stories to tell of escapes, executions and famous men.[37]

These stories were often related from first-hand experience. Indeed, it should be noted that the Chairman of the Committee, Seamus Brennan (who was to become a prominent figure in the eventual restoration project at the jail), was himself under sentence of death in the prison in 1916.

As a result of the proceeds of the day, a memorial to Seán Heuston was eventually erected in the Phoenix Park.[38] Pressure on the government for action at Kilmainham continued. An excellent documentary film on the jail was produced by the Educational Film Company of Ireland, with a script by a former political prisoner Margaret Buckley.[39]

Another open day took place in June, when Éamon de Valera and some cabinet ministers (many of whom were former prisoners themselves) were among the many visitors.[40] The government interest in the jail was apparently sincere, but there was also a strong consciousness of public spending. The country was only beginning to emerge from an economic war and there was a pronounced reluctance to commit to what seemed like costly schemes and projects. There was a consciousness of the investment in the war memorial garden in nearby Islandbridge, which was now almost complete. Remembering the Irish who were killed during the First World War while serving in the British army was a controversial issue, but de Valera's government had made the magnanimous gesture of committing to the project and the memorial garden, designed by the renowned British architect Edwin Lutyens, was laid out from 1933-8 at a not inconsiderable cost to the state. There were also exciting but very expensive plans to develop Leinster House, the National Library, the National Museum, the National Art Gallery and the Natural History Museum as one great, world-class cultural centre.[41] As regards 1916 and the struggle for independence, there already was a popular National Rising's Collection in the National Museum. De Valera had presented the museum with an ornamental 1916 role of honour, which had become a central part of the Rising's collection on permanent display.

SEAN HEUSTON
Executed in Kilmainham Jail, May 8th, 1916.

Souvenir

OF

Your Visit

TO

Kilmainham Jail

Sunday, 20th March, 1938

Far left: The Seán Heuston Committee open day at the jail attracted enormous numbers.

Above: Group paying respects in the stonebreaker's yard, Seán Heuston Committee open day.

Left: The statue of Seán Heuston, unveiled in the Phoenix Park in 1943.

Taoiseach Éamon de Valera and members of his cabinet visiting Kilmainham Jail, in June 1938, during an open day organised by the Easter Week Men's Association.

The determination of Fianna Fáil to cling to the 1916 mantle was manifested in the elaborate commemorations held in 1935. An Easter Week Memorial Committee, established by de Valera, organised the first state military parade and march by the National army and 1916 veterans (a number of whom would later be actively involved in the restoration of Kilmainham Jail) through the main thoroughfares of Dublin, which was followed by the unveiling of an official memorial of the 1916 Rising. De Valera's ability to manipulate nationalist ideology to his advantage was evident in his salvaging of an old piece of sculpture which had been languishing unsold in the studio of a sculptor, Oliver Sheppard, for some twenty years. A bronze cast was made of the figure depicting the death of Cúchulainn and it was unveiled after the parade in the General Post Office. The base, made of Connemara marble, featured a bronze plaque recording the 1916 Proclamation. At the official unveiling ceremony, de Valera provided the ideological interpretation of the piece:

Everyone who enters this hall henceforth will be reminded of the deed enacted here. A beautiful piece of sculpture, the creation of Irish genius, symbolising the dauntless courage and abiding constancy of our people will commemorate it modestly but fittingly.

The use of the word 'modest' is interesting. De Valera also introduced a public ceremony at Arbour Hill, where the 1916 leaders are buried. The site was soon made accessible to the public on a daily basis. It may have seemed that enough was being done to commemorate Ireland's patriotic dead. The government were considering the creation of a public park by the Rotunda Hospital to commemorate those who died in the struggle for independence.[42] The sum necessary to restore Kilmainham Jail would have seemed large. These were factors which at least hindered progress.

4

PROCRASTINATION

Further considerations of the proposals for use of the jail were completely dropped in 1939 following the outbreak of war in Europe.[43] This did not deter Seán Fitzpatrick from writing to the Board of Works, pleading the case of the 'large number of Old IRA men who are unemployed and on the brink of starvation [who] could be usefully engaged cleaning the outside and inside of the old jail which is in a filthy condition'.[44]

With the ending of the Second World War and thus of the Emergency period in Ireland in 1945, the government found itself under no major pressure to restore the jail. In 1946, the Department of Posts and Telegraphs and the Department of Finance both enquired as to the possibility of the premises being adapted for office accommodation.[45]

The CPW advised that such an adaptation could not be carried out at a reasonable cost, and that the premises were, in any event, unsuitable for that purpose. In July 1946, the government directed that the Minister for Finance should further examine the question of the future of the jail:

> ... and should submit to the government proposals for the preservation of the buildings to the maximum extent that might be feasible and desirable, regard being had to considerations of historic interest and to the possibilities of utilising portions of the buildings for State purposes.[46]

Following consultation with the Department of Defence, draft plans were prepared by the CPW to utilise the premises as a Defence Museum. In this scheme, the museum would occupy the former main hall building and the plan would involve demolishing the partition walls between the cells in order to make a more effective museum space. A block containing a curator's residence and caretaker's quarters would be erected around the present entrance, and the boundary walls on the east, west and south sides would be lowered. Excluding the memorial park previously suggested by the National Graves Association, the cost was estimated at £90,000.[47]

At the same time, the Public Records Office asked for additional storage accommodation, and the suggestions put forward included the adaptation of Kilmainham Jail:

… giving 15,000ft of shelving; the estimated cost being £75,000 minimum. This scheme would involve the restoration of the Main Hall and surrounding cells and of the Governor's house and entrance, the provision of a new wing at one end of the main hall for stairs, lifts, office and sanitary accommodation, and the demolition of the remaining buildings.[48]

This proposal, however, (as well as that for a Defence Museum) was not accepted, mainly on the grounds of the costs involved.[49]

This continuing unsatisfactory situation was raised in the Dáil on 21 May 1946, when Peadar Doyle, the Parliamentary Secretary to the Minister for Finance, was asked what the proposals were regarding the jail. He replied, 'The only thing I can tell you about it at the moment is that we are finding considerable difficulty in arriving at a decision as to what it is practicable to do in connection with it. No final decision has been made as yet.'[50] The situation had not changed by 1948, when the Fianna Fáil party was replaced in office by a new coalition government that did not express any interest in developing Kilmainham Jail. Only when Fianna Fáil returned to government in 1951 did the issue arise again.

Proposals were once again considered by the de Valera government. Wide interpretations of the planned 'historical' museum intended for Kilmainham were occasionally made. Michael Quane, who was responsible for the Transport Section of the CPW, wrote enthusiastically:

As our collections of coaches, &c., which are now widely separated in storage in Co. Kilkenny, Co. Sligo and the Royal Hospital properly belong to a historical museum, I take it that you will consider the question of including these (and perhaps others of our collections) in the material intended for the new museum.[51]

Quane's proposal would have required much renovation of the existing building just to get the vehicles inside. The government, however, stood by the original intention of preserving as much of the structure as possible and Quane's hopes were dashed.

In August 1953, the Cabinet Committee on the Provision of Employment decided that the jail should be converted to a museum with a small memorial park and that with this adaptation no permanent structure or wall would be removed.[52] On 28 August, a press release was issued confirming that, 'The government have recently decided that Kilmainham Jail should be preserved as a national monument, and the necessary steps to that end are being put in place.'[53] The news was heralded with prominent articles in all of the national papers. *The Irish Press* ran the headline, 'Kilmainham Jail to be Preserved'.[54] It certainly appeared that the jail had been saved and that its future was secured at last.

But the depressing economic realities took their toll and the restoration work at Kilmainham did not begin immediately. Using the jail restoration as a job-creation scheme was considered – akin to the earlier NGA proposal – but the scheme was not set into motion. Wider economic and social problems continued to mount for the government, and in 1954 Fianna Fáil was once again out of power. The new coalition government included the Labour Party, and one of its members, Mr O'Leary, quickly made the party position on Kilmainham very clear in the Dáil on 15 June:

> We believe that the spending of money on Constellations[55] and on schemes such as the building of the Bray Road, Kilmainham Jail and on new government buildings should cease. We believe that all these schemes were nonsense and should not have been introduced by Fianna Fáil. I often wonder how Deputy de Valera allowed his party to introduce them.[56]

A Fianna Fáil response to Mr O'Leary's remarks was made later by Seán Lemass:

> I hope that the decision to establish a historical museum in Kilmainham Jail will not be scotched. That building is there. It is falling into disrepair and becoming an eyesore for want of upkeep. It has considerable historical associations, and it is an appropriate place for such a museum. That there should be a museum will, I think, be accepted by most Deputies. At the present time there is completely inadequate accommodation for many historical objects and souvenirs, which should be on display ... The pressure on the National Museum could be greatly relieved if this project for an historical museum in Kilmainham Jail is allowed to proceed. The advantage of having additional attractions of that kind in Dublin from the point of view of our tourist trade is also worth bearing in mind.[57]

5

MALAISE

Lemass's words of wisdom were not heeded, and still nothing was done. In 1956, Dublin Corporation made an order granting special permission for the erection of a cinema on the grounds immediately adjoining Kilmainham Jail. The CPW lodged an appeal against the order with the Minister for Local Government, given that the jail, both on historical and aesthetic grounds, had every qualification to be considered an important national monument. Referring to the various plans to use the jail for museum purposes the council concluded, 'Bearing in mind these considerations the council strongly recommend that the entire amenity land of the Jail, including the site of the proposed cinema, be acquired by the commissioners for the State.'[58] Although planning was forbidden for the cinema, the surrounding land was not purchased.[59]

By this stage the CPW had already decided not to allow any more groups access to the jail building, as there was a constant danger of falling slates, glass and plaster, with unsafe roofs and timber floors. As a letter to the Department of Finance explained:

> Normally, we have been accustomed to refuse permission to members of the public to visit the jail … we have allowed visits in exceptional cases, subject to the applicants signing a form of indemnity against accidents. In view, however, of our architect's report we do not propose to permit any further such visits. As this may possibly give rise to protests and representations to members of the government, we have considered it well to report the matter at this stage for the information of the minister for finance.[60]

With the future of the jail now seemingly more at risk than ever, Fianna Fáil returned to office in 1957. The economy had now hit an all-time low and the restoration of the jail was not a priority on the agenda. Nonetheless, the first of a series of restoration programmes was begun in the nearby Royal Hospital Kilmainham, a former hospital for retired soldiers who had served in the British army. As regards nationalist commemoration, what was considered a significant investment was made to develop a fitting memorial to the 1916 leaders at their place of burial in Arbour Hill. The CPW had begun the transformation of

Boy looking into the abandoned jail, early 1950s.

the environment of the graves with new lawns, paved terraces and a memorial in 1952, but the scheme dragged on into the late 1950s, proving more costly than had been originally anticipated. There was also, at this time, a financial commitment by the State to develop a garden of remembrance in Parnell Square and a large site was purchased on the northern side of the square for this purpose.[61] These commitments must have been a factor in the further prolongation of inactivity on the Kilmainham Jail front.

Though the depressing lack of progress on the issue continued, it was obvious there were still some people with serious concern for the jail. Perhaps this helps to explain why *The Sunday Press* broke with an unsubstantiated but highly dramatic story of one man, Patrick J. Stephenson (Dublin City Librarian, Honorary Secretary of the Old Dublin Society and 1916 veteran), and his fight against apparent proposals to pull down the jail. The title was deliberately provocative:

An abominable betrayal of every Irish patriot who walked the land from Henry Joy McCracken to Kevin Barry. Those are the fighting words of a fighting Irishman when telling *The Sunday Press* – and the nation – what he thinks of proposals to pull down Kilmainham Jail.[62]

The article makes no further mention of these 'proposals' but instead focuses on Stephenson:

In his book-lined office in Pearse Street he detailed the plans that will make Kilmainham the capital's historic showpiece for thousands of tourists a year on a par with the *Invalides* in Paris and the Tower of London and other historic places of pilgrimage. He visualised all the national relics, mementoes, documents, guns, etc., now scattered throughout the city, dramatically arranged in Kilmainham's cells to provide a national museum in every sense of the word.[63]

Exterior of the jail in the early 1950s.

Although the article, in fact, made no new suggestions, it did reintroduce vital ingredients – popular awareness and interest in the jail, as well as a desperately needed injection of urgency, pressure and drama into the situation. At last a change was in the air.

6

VOLUNTARY SPIRIT

Whereas Patrick Stephenson provided the necessary voice, the real individual who deserves credit for finally ensuring something would be done with the jail was another member of the Old Dublin Society, Lorcan Leonard. From early in the 1950s he had discussed the possibility of restoring Kilmainham as a museum with various people. As he was later to write:

> I met Paddy Stephenson one night at a meeting of the Old Dublin Society and during the course of a few drinks after the meeting I got the promise of his support for any action I might take or organise short of 'mass action' to preserve the jail. He said that within a few years he would be out on pension and then he wouldn't give a damn what action was taken.[64]

Stephenson duly contributed a short article and a talk on the need to restore Kilmainham Jail to the *Dublin Historical Record* in 1957. He also later invited the historian A.J. Nowlan to give a lecture on the history of Kilmainham Jail. In the summer of 1958, Leonard made a draft of a plan of restoration, based on voluntary labour, which would turn the jail into a historical museum. Stephenson supported his plans and it was decided 'to call a meeting of some people who would be interested and who by their "records" would add weight to our eventual petition to the government'.[65] Leonard most notably sent a letter to Seán Dowling, Chairman of the Old IRA Literary and Debating Society, looking for the support of that organisation:

> I write to you on behalf of myself and Mr P.J. Stephenson that you may submit to your committee or council, our request for support and/or help in an effort to save Kilmainham Jail from the ravages of time and the indifference of politicians. It is our intention to get a committee to plan a real campaign to restore Kilmainham Jail and arrange the prison as a Historical Museum, and principally, to elevate that weed-grown, debris-strewn yard of which you are aware, to the most holy spot in Ireland.
>
> You have probably heard that there are plans afoot to demolish the jail and it will be done as soon as somebody from the Board of Works says it is beyond all repair. What was once a

monument to heroic endeavour is now the silent mocking cavern to the indifferences of our times. There is a great urgency in this matter and we would appreciate the submission of this letter to your Council as soon as possible. Finally we would suggest that if the support of your council is forthcoming, a representative of your Council should join the committee we propose.

Leonard's next step was to book a room in Jury's Hotel, Dublin, in September 1958 and to invite all those interested in discussing his restoration project.[66] Although a little sceptical at first, the Old IRA Association decided to offer their full support, provided 'nothing of or relating to the period after 1921 would be identified with the Kilmainham project'. This suited Leonard's intentions. He was also aware of the excellent recruiting potential among the Old IRA.[67] With sufficient gravitas now provided, a provisional committee was formed. Many notable figures were also happy to offer their support: Seán MacBride, Peadar O'Donnell, Tom Barry, Florrie O'Donoghue, Todd Andrews, Cathal O'Shannon, Maurice Twomey, Dan Breen, Donagh McDonagh, Margaret Pearse and the now very elderly former secretary of the NGA, Seán Fitzpatrick. In addition, Leonard secured a basic acceptance of his plans for the voluntary project from the Building Trades Council and the Congress of Irish Trade Unions.

Lorcan Leonard, the main force behind the restoration of the jail.

Kilmainham Jail

By A. J. NOWLAN

Read to the Old Dublin Society on 10th March, 1958.

IN Ireland, as indeed in other countries, during medieval days a custom prevailed of using gate towers as prisons. On the picturesque slopes of Kilmainham to the west of the present Royal Hospital and to the north of the Courthouse and Jail, the Hospitallers of St. John of Jerusalem built the Great House or Castle of Kilmainham about 1212. Here the Irish Prior with his staff of Knights, Squires, Chaplains and Attendants dwelt for 360 years until the Suppression of the Monasteries. Within the quadrangle of this stately edifice were various buildings including a prison, *tetra domus de Malrepos*, " the dismal house of Little-ease ".[1] In succeeding years a Manor Court prison, a Bridewell, a Penitentiary, a Women's Penitentiary and a County Jail were situated in the Kilmainham district.

Towards the end of the eighteenth century a new County Jail was erected which in turn became a State Prison and continued as such until modern times.

This paper is a contribution to the history of Kilmainham Jail from its erection in 1796 until it was vested in the General Prisons Board in 1878 as a State Prison. The material presented has been collected from such official and unofficial sources as I have been able to examine.

At the outset it is necessary to review the circumstances which led to the construction of the new County Jail on its present site to replace the old one.

In the latter part of the 18th century public opinion in various countries was aroused at the appalling jail conditions and a campaign started for the introduction of a more enlightened system firstly by substituting imprisonment for the death penalty in less serious offences, and secondly by improving prisons.[2]

John Howard, a noted philanthropist and widely travelled prison reformer who visited Dublin in 1779, attributed the overcrowded conditions in our city prisons to the current practice of detaining acquitted prisoners until they had paid the iniquitous fees charged by the Clerk of the Crown or Peace, Sheriff, Gaoler or Turnkey.[3] The system of extorting such fees originated in medieval times and had been confirmed by a Statute of 1634 limiting the amounts which could be demanded.[4] At Kilmainham he was appalled at the fees system in operation and secured the release of some youths by paying half the fees. He also paid the fees for 15 acquitted adults whom he considered deserving cases, thus restoring them to their families.[5]

The County Jail at that time was situated on the low portion of Old Kilmainham which is referred to in the Ordnance Survey Name Book as " Kilmainham Lane Old, on the Cork and Waterford Road, running East and West, beginning at Mount Brown ". The site is shown on the 1911 edition of the 25" Ordnance Survey Map (sheet 18Xb) and was opposite the present Brookfield Road, where it joins Old Kilmainham.

In June 1784 the gaoler intercepted two men trying to escape and secured them " as well as the wretched jail he keeps would admit of ". There were then 64 prisoners immured in three small underground dungeons with a grating fronting the road through which they appealed to passers by for food, liquor and instruments to escape, and loudly rebuked those who would not assist them. The report added : " There was not so weak or ill conceived a jail as the County Dublin one, and it was hoped that a new one would be built on a proper construction and site ".[6]

Following consultations with some interested county gentlemen the Grand Jury of the County Dublin arranged to have a plan prepared for a new and commodious jail which it was hoped would serve as a model for similar structures about to be rebuilt in various parts of the country. The plan was approved by the Grand Jury in Michaelmas Term, 1785. It now remained

A *Dublin Historical Record* article on the jail by A.J. Nowlan.

In the meantime, government plans for the jail appeared to be backtracking somewhat. At a meeting of the government held on 1 July 1958, the Minister for Finance suggested, on the advice of the CPW, that instead of carrying into effect the decision taken by the Cabinet Committee on the Provision of Employment on 26 August 1953, 'it would be better to remove what is left of the roofs, repair and cap the walls, preserve some of the cells, preserve the whole of the then remaining structure as a national monument and restore and maintain the plots'.[68] In other words, the jail would not, in fact, be adopted for use as a museum, 'a purpose for which it would, in any event be unsuitable'.[69] It was decided that that the Tánaiste and the Ministers for Health, Finance and Agriculture would inspect Kilmainham Jail and that suggestions made by the CPW in regard to the jail would be further considered in the light of the views formed by those Ministers.[70]

While government officials prepared for yet another inspection, a meeting of the Old IRA Literary and Debating Society in the Mansion House had George Tully talk to them about Kilmainham Jail. The essence of his message was to convert Kilmainham into a national monument so that 'a visit to it will convey to the young mind more of the character of our long revolution than might be got from a dozen history books'.[71] As a result of the lecture, a letter on behalf of the society was written directly to de Valera:

> There is a craving for knowledge of local and national history waiting to be satisfied, and where better in a properly organised museum than in Kilmainham, make it the capital's showpiece for our people and as a tourist attraction. Make that stone-breaking yard where our leaders died a Garden of Remembrance.
>
> We look forward to the day when the gaunt pile will be converted into a place of National Pilgrimage, where the story of Ireland's long fight for freedom could be told better than in any history books.[72]

A few days after this letter was written, a report was submitted by the Minister for Finance from the inspection of the jail by the four Ministers, calling for the CPW to furnish an estimate of the cost of a modified proposal as soon as possible.[73] Meanwhile, Seamus Brennan finally received a reply from de Valera's secretary on 20 December 1958, only to inform him that the position regarding Kilmainham Jail was receiving careful consideration. The matter was raised in the Dáil on 3 March 1959 and again on 12 May, with the unconvincing assurance given on both occasions that the matter was being actively pursued and that a statement would be made as soon as practicable.

As the procrastination by the government continued, the Kilmainham Jail Restoration Committee (KJRC) obtained permission from the CPW to carry out an inspection of the jail prior to submitting plans for restoration. As Lorcan Leonard later recorded:

> On a wet Saturday in November 1959 the Provisional Committee, at least those members who were constantly attending meetings, made an inspection of the site and with us came Dermot

O'Toole and Fergus Clarke who I had recruited to give the committee any architectural or structural advice when desired.[74]

After the visit, Leonard immediately set about preparing the project proposal, which was submitted two weeks later.[75] On 28 January 1960, the Minister of Finance,[76] accompanied by the Parliamentary Secretary, received a deputation of four representatives of the committee to discuss the proposed scheme. Whereas the Minister outlined the government plans for partial restoration of the jail, the KJRC stated that they aimed at complete restoration and were prepared to go ahead on that basis, subject to the conditions that the government might lay down:

> The Committee also stressed that they had been promised some supplies of materials free of charge and that they were very hopeful of being able to raise by their own efforts the funds needed to meet the cost of such supplies of materials as would have to be purchased.[77]

The Minister was impressed by the proposals, and with a few extra provisos[78] was prepared to recommend a five-year lease of the jail (at a nominal rent of one penny a year) to the committee.[79] With the Department of Education also approving the proposal, a government meeting held on 26 February 1960 saw the Kilmainham Jail Provisional Committee's project officially approved.[80] Among some of the older government ministers there was surely a measure of relief to have the fate of the jail finally settled. Perhaps some were pleased to have the matter out of their hands at last. Care of the 'national shrine' would now be someone else's responsibility.

7

RESTORATION PROPOSAL ACCEPTED

The KJRC were informed one week after the government meeting that a slightly modified version of their proposals to restore the jail would be accepted.[81] In compliance with the terms of agreement a Board of Trustees was duly formed. There were seven Trustees, two of whom, Frank Thornton and Lt-Col. Matt Feehan, were appointed by the Minister for Finance (both were 1916 veterans). The other five were Mrs Nora Connolly O'Brien (daughter of James Connolly and a former Kilmainham prisoner herself), Seán Dowling, Joseph Groome, Daniel F. Stephenson (son of P.J. Stephenson) and Éamon Martin (another 1916 veteran). With the final details of the agreement settled, one month later the news was issued to the press on 29 April. The following day *The Irish Press* featured a prominent article with an old title: 'Kilmainham is Saved'.[82]

On 2 May the Committee made a public appeal for funds and stated that they would appeal later for voluntary labour, equipment and materials. As the restoration committee enthusiastically prepared to begin, there were those who had criticisms. The new leader of the Labour party, Brendan Corish, made objections in the Dáil on 17 May 1960 to the idea of voluntary labour being used for the project. James Brennan, a Fianna Fáil TD, replied in the Dáil:

> I was sorry that Deputy Corish saw fit to make a kind of adverse criticism on the question of voluntary labour. Whether or not one agrees with the propriety of voluntary labour, I think it is one case where sentiment and patriotism should transcend any other consideration ... If this committee succeeds in restoring the jail as a national monument, and preserving it as an historical museum, it will be one of the greatest monuments we have. There are very excellent people on this committee, people prompted by nothing more than the highest ideals of patriotism. They deserve the full support of everyone who has any interest at all in the struggle that took place down through the years for freedom.[83]

Three days after Brennan's speech the Trustees of KJRC signed a five-year lease on Kilmainham Jail with the CPW at Groome's Hotel in Dublin and the jail was thereby officially handed over to the Trustee Committee. On Saturday 21 May 1960, after formally receiving the keys from a CPW official, the committee entered the jail and the restoration work could finally begin.[84] As *The Irish Press* recorded one week later:

> … already the workmen of Dublin, the builders, carpenters, glaziers, plumbers and others – a full 60 of them were busy beginning the task of restoration. From now on such voluntary labour will be found in Kilmainham Jail on Saturday afternoons, on ordinary holidays, during the long daylight hours of summer, carrying out this labour of patriotism until it is completed. Dublin firms have made the first gifts of bricks, glass, cement, and other building materials, and one also have given the necessary tubular scaffolding.[85]

Kilmainham Jail Trustees signing the lease at Groome's Hotel, May 1960. Standing, left to right: Lt-Col. Matt Feehan, Daniel Stephenson, Lorcan Leonard, Eoin O'Keefe, Stephen Murphy, Eamon Martin. Seated, left to right: Eamon de Barra, Seamus Brennan, Seán Dowling, Frank Thornton, Nora Connolly O'Brien.

Seán Dowling entering the jail after receiving the keys from an OPW official, 21 May 1960.

Site inspection and tour being led by Seamus Brennan, 21 May 1960.

Among the many contributions, Roadstone Ltd donated mortar and sand, Protim gave wood preservative, Irish Wire products gave nails, Denis Guiney provided overalls and uniforms for the workers, Davies & Co. provided cement and lime, McQuillan & Co. provided tools, the McHenry Brothers (one a former Kilmainham prisoner) provided turf briquettes as well as a vital collection and delivery service with their truck to the volunteers, Joseph McGrath (another former Kilmainham prisoner, later of Irish Sweepstakes and *Artic Prince* fame) provided gas heating, and, under unrelenting duress, the forestry division of the Department of Lands donated timber. The windows of the infirmary building were reglazed by the generosity and interest of the Dublin Glass & Paint Company. Other sundry items were donated, such as sanitary materials, desks, heaters and chairs. The workers' canteen, which was quickly established in the old infirmary of the jail,[86] was not forgotten about. The volunteers received donations of cigarettes, jam for sandwiches and dairy products.

Above left: Roofless former Catholic chapel of the jail in 1960.

Above right: View of a jail yard giving an indication of the formidable amount of work which had to be done to restore the jail.

Above left: Yard of the jail in 1960.

Above right: A wall of the jail in 1960.

South-west corner of the jail in 1960.

Volunteers get to work.

When the work of restoration commenced, the condition of the building was such that many parts could not be entered without danger, and every roof was open to the sky. The stone floor of the central hall was a foot deep in earth and:

> … a lavish growth of ferns, weeds and even young trees were flourishing. In the various exercise yards nature had taken undisturbed control and more than twenty trees up to forty feet high had to be felled as well as hundreds of saplings.[87]

There was also, in many places, a dense undergrowth of brambles and thorn bushes, often four to five feet high.[88]

Practically all the cells in the central compound had the plaster hanging off the walls and ceilings, if not strewn all over the floor, 'Every gutter and every window was broken, iron stairways were rusted through, timber rotted away. Ivy had crept through the windows and spread over the walls.'[89] It should also be noted that the site was infested with pigeons, rats and other vermin. The volunteers undoubtedly faced a very formidable challenge.[90]

The first task of the site committee was to clear the yards and open areas so that access could be gained to the basement under the central compound, the infirmary, and the governor's quarters. As Lorcan Leonard has vividly recorded:

Every available man went into the attack with axes, bush-saws and grappling tools, and within a short time a path had been cut around the south, east and north areas of the jail. When this area was accessible and the buildings examined, the following broad plan of action was decided upon.

1. Complete the clearing and cleaning of all yards.
2. Lay-in temporary water service and electric light.
3. Demolish what remained of the roof over the east wing of the '98 jail.
4. Demolish the roof and intermediate floors of the governor's quarters.
5. Set up stores and joiners' shop at the west end of the Administration wing.
6. Convert infirmary into administration offices.
7. Clear all cells of '98 section of fallen plaster and debris.

This work went ahead through June, July, August and September. By the end of July fires were blazing in the yards, burning the fallen trees, brambles and ivy, with flames and smoke shooting higher than the old walls. On one occasion some worried citizen on the Emmet Road summoned the police, and in due course the squad cars arrived at the jail gates inquiring if we needed assistance, we did, but not what they had to offer.[91]

A volunteer removing weeds.

Dublin bricklayer Pat Brown offering his services.

Joe Maguill, a Belfastman, and caretaker of the jail for many years, fixing slates on the roof of the prison.

Left: John Hanratty, a member of the Irish Citizen Army in 1916, here aged eighty, working on the roof of the jail.

Below: Volunteer workers on the roof of the east wing. Note the absence of safety harnesses, etc. They are at a very considerable height. Despite the evident risks, there were no very serious injuries incurred by any of the workers.

Distinguished members of the KJRS at rest: From left: unknown to author, John Hanratty, Simon Donnolly, unknown to author, Peter O'Connor, Seamus Brennan.

Opposite above: Volunteers taking a break in the canteen, which was established in the old infirmary of the jail.

Opposite below: Female volunteers in the canteen.

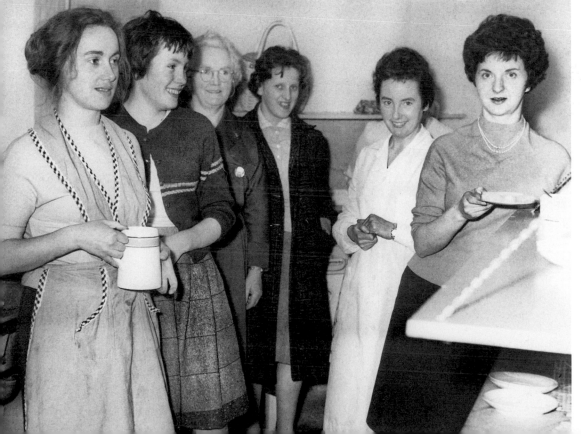

Group of volunteers giving an indication of the wide age range of the workers.

HELP

THE KILMAINHAM JAIL RESTORATION SOCIETY

WHO ARE RESTORING THE JAIL BY VOLUNTARY EFFORT AS A NATIONAL MONUMENT TO THE DEAD WHO DIED FOR IRELAND.

The KJRS did not fail to get the message out in the early years.

Young volunteers painting in the east wing. Experience and connections gained while working in the jail helped a number of young men obtain work in trades with the OPW and Dublin Corporation.

Above: Members of the Old IRA Debating Society – almost all of the above were members of the KJRS: From left (front) George Tully, Seamus Brennan, John Hanratty, N. Laffan, Stephen Murphy. Back Row (from left) P. Young, C. Moore, Rita Dorr, P. Buttner, Stephen O'Neill.

Left: Kilmainham Calling!

Opposite above: Press article on the jail giving an indication of sympathy and support.

Opposite below: Press profiles of four volunteers.

AN ANSWER TO THE 'WHAT'S IN IT FOR ME JACK' BRIGADE

THE SUNDAY PRESS, APRIL 23, 1961

Shining example in this age of cynicism

WALKING in the April air of space age, with the sun shining, it is an anachronism. The walls are mocked by Today and its Tomorrow with all the tremendous unborn things of its womb. But walk inside the shadow of the tall walls of Kilmainham Gaol even in this April and Yesterday...

Mr. Joe Magill, 220 St. Peter's road, Walkinstown, has been working at Kilmainham for the past 12 months.

Mr. Raymond Cassidy, Thorncastle street, Ringsend.

Dominick Cassidy, Thorncastle street, Ringsend, one of the volunteer workers rebuilding Kilmainham Gaol.

Mr. John Hanratty, 139 Clonliffe road, Drumcondra, has been at work in Kilmainham since the reconstruction project began.

EVENING HERALD 2/3/61

SUNDAY PRESS 4/3/61

Jail museum articles for exhibition in Dublin

Herald Staff Reporter
exhibition of documents, arms, pictures and other es intended for the Kilmainham Jail Museum will be opened...

Dublin Exhibition will tell of nation's Fight for Freedom

George Tully (far right) with two other volunteers cleaning over the front portal of the jail.

Early visitors to the jail. By October 1960, large numbers of visitors were being admitted to see the jail.

8

ENTHUSIASM ABOUNDS

From the earliest stage the enthusiasm of the voluntary workers was strikingly evident. At a meeting of the supporters of the project in October (after almost five months of restoration work) at the Mansion House, Seán Dowling remarked that since the voluntary work had started, the workers had put in 9,000 hours at the jail. There was by now a panel of 250 voluntary workers, drawn from a very wide variety of trades and professions. The project seemed to inspire a form of patriotic duty among many. As *The Irish Press* noted:

> One man had spent his two-week holidays on the job. A Dublin worker in Birmingham was subscribing 10/- a month. [Seán] Dowling also outlined plans to organise committees in Belfast, Cork, Galway, Limerick, Waterford and elsewhere to obtain financial support. It was also intended to appeal to various firms to contribute towards the project. Lorcan Leonard said that when they went in, parts of the jail were like a jungle. Over 200,000 tons of debris had been removed from the site.[92]

By October 1960, it was deemed that the jail was safe enough to allow visitors and it was soon estimated that approximately 300 people were visiting the jail every weekend.

Apart from their success in founding committees around Ireland, as well as one in London, the KJRS quickly proved particularly adept at fundraising. A remarkable number of letters were sent out to various organisations, looking for financial support.[93] The Irish Georgian Society was one of the early contributors. Commercial and industrial firms were asked to donate 100 guineas for the restoration of a cell. Soon, donations were coming in from many countrymen's associations and from such unexpected sources such as Queen's University, Belfast.[94] In the early months of 1961, the committee was provided with rooms at the Carlisle Buildings in Dublin (beside O'Connell Bridge), for use as an information bureau and as a recruiting centre for volunteers.

On St Patrick's Day 1961, an exhibition on the jail, featuring numerous items of historical interest, was launched in the Carlisle Buildings.[95] Included in the exhibition were original paintings by Jack B. Yeats, Seán O'Sullivan, Harry Kernoff and Maurice

MacGonigal, portrait busts by Albert Power, Joseph Cashman's collection of historical photographs, selections from the Lawrence and Cooke collections, and photostatic copies of Kilmainham Jail registers. In the first weekend, over 1,500 people visited the exhibition and contributed their shillings to the restoration fund. The exhibition ran for over three months at that venue, before being relocated to the Building Centre, Baggot Street, where it remained for over two years and helped provide a considerable amount of finance to the committee. On the 7 May 1961, a concert was held at the Gaiety Theatre in Dublin in aid of the KJRC.[96] Among those performing were Bernadette Greevy and Brendan Kavanagh. The concert was attended by the Taoiseach, Seán Lemass, who had already provided the committee with a generous personal donation.[97] Another Dublin function held at this time to assist the restoration was a Céilí Dance at the Irish Club, Parnell Square.

Alongside collections and activities being held at various venues in Dublin, there were also fundraising activities much further afield. On 7 September the London Committee of the Kilmainham Jail restoration project held a fundraising event in Lambeth Town Hall, featuring 'The Irish Army with Pipers and bands, dignitaries of church and State, Tara Céilí Band, Cuirim Ceoil, the Gaelic League Choir and more.'[98]

Left: Members of the All-Ireland winning Down team visiting the jail, September 1961. Left to right: Maurice Hayes (Secretary, Down County Board), James McCartan, Dan McCartan, Kevin O'Neill).

Opposite above: Group from Queen's University, Belfast with the Lord Mayor of Dublin, Bob Briscoe (third from left), visiting the jail.

Opposite below: De Valera visiting the cell in which he was held after the Civil War, with the former Governor of the jail, William Corri, in 1962. It was an amicable re-acquaintance. In the early years of the restoration the Civil War was very rarely mentioned by guides and there was a general agreement to leave behind Civil War animosities.

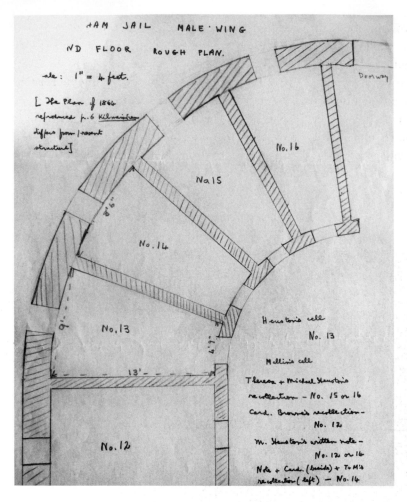

Page from a letter written by a relative of Sean Heuston, outlining the exact cell Heuston was held in. It quickly became possible to identify a large number of cells occupied by notable political prisoners in this way.

Meanwhile the restoration work continued apace and increasing number of visitors were permitted to receive a guided tour around the jail on Sundays, sometimes conducted by a former prisoner. In late September 1961, the morning after the All-Ireland football final, the victorious County Down team were provided with a tour of the jail as part of a sightseeing trip through the city. The losing County Offaly team visited the jail in the afternoon.[99]

Some visitors to the prison made significant donations to the KJRC. One American lady visitor was sufficiently inspired by the project to donate £2,000. Contributions were also facilitated by the purchase of a short publication on the history of the jail, *Kilmainham Jail, The Bastille of Ireland* (illustrated with drawings by Maurice MacGonigal and others), which was published in 1961.[100] Another publication, *The Ghosts of Kilmainham* soon followed. The year also saw the KJRC officially inaugurated as a limited company, The Kilmainham Jail Restoration Society (KJRS).

In November, the society entertained a large gathering of members to a film show at the jail. The films, *A visit to Kilmainham*, produced by the Brothers O'Connor, *Progress of the restoration work*, produced by a Mr Crowe, and *The Patriot*, a documentary on Kevin Barry produced by T. Murphy, were all the work of members of the society. During the evening, members stated their intention to hold further similar functions, lectures, etc.

The society then began to feel sufficiently confident to advance plans for a museum in the jail. On 28 March 1962, a Museum Committee was formally constituted to collect museum material and arrange for its storage, preservation and exhibition in the jail; the material exhibited to illustrate in particular the period from 1796 until the closing of the jail in 1924, but not to exclude any material, relating to any period, illustrative of the fight of the Irish people for independence.

Simon Donnelly, a prisoner in Kilmainham in 1921, identifying the cell in which he was held.

Shortly before the temporary exhibition in the Building Centre finished, it was visited by the Taoiseach, Seán Lemass.[101] He was met on arrival by members of the restoration committee and he showed a keen interest in the pictures and manuscripts. Before leaving, he was presented with a specially bound souvenir copy of the history of the jail by Mr D. Stephenson. Mr Lemass told reporters, 'I hope that in this time left to see it many people will come to this extraordinary exhibition. The organisers deserve great credit for bringing such very interesting photographs and historical documents together.'[102]

The committee soon gathered a very impressive body of exhibits, including an original 1916 Proclamation, various original letters written by some of the famous inmates, and a wide range of other memorabilia. As the donations continued to flow in, the expanding collection eventually became a serious concern to the National Museum, the Director of which, Dr O'Sullivan, felt compelled to contact the Taoiseach's office over the matter. As Lemass's secretary recorded:

> He [O'Sullivan] is perturbed by the situation that is being created by the establishment of an historical museum at Kilmainham Jail. He has no objection to the establishment of the museum, and the National Museum have already given the organisers of the project considerable assistance, but the stage is now being reached where we will have two separate institutions competing for items of historical interest. Already a nephew of Miss Pearse has advised the National Museum that he proposes to withdraw certain items for deposit in Kilmainham. Dr O'Sullivan wondered whether the government had expressed any views on the development of Kilmainham Jail as a Museum.[103]

Lemass's sympathies were, however, inclined towards the KJRS. On 3 May 1964, he paid a visit to the jail 'where he was kept as a boy in his teens for his part in the 1916 Rising'.[104] Lemass was taken on a tour of the prison and viewed some of the many items of historical interest which had been collected by the society.

9

GROWING CONFIDENCE

The sheer confidence of the KJRS at this stage was remarkable. The previous August, James Brennan had written to Lord Killanin, Honorary Consul for Monaco, in advance of Princess Grace and Prince Rainier's visit to Ireland, to suggest that a visit to the jail be included on their itinerary:

> If Her Serene Highness were to agree to come to the jail, while we would ensure that there would, as I said, be no advance publicity, we would like to be able to publish, afterwards, a photograph of her while there.[105]

Although Princess Grace, who attracted great crowds everywhere she went in Ireland (and who was of a proud Irish background), may have found a visit to Kilmainham interesting, the invitation was not taken up.

Another world figure who might have visited Kilmainham at this time was the President of the United States, John F. Kennedy. In this case the invitation had perhaps more realistic possibilities. The American Embassy in Dublin actually wrote to the KJRS enquiring as to whether there was any political prisoner held in the jail with the name Kennedy, who might be a relation of the President.[106] Despite careful study of the records the committee simply could not find evidence of such a person. Perhaps the greatest publicity opportunity the jail would ever have thus slipped away.[107]

Despite receiving occasional knocks, the KJRS battled on and spirits remained very high. By 1964, the building had been re-roofed and the major restoration work was by now, with some exceptions, complete. The society had been successful in attaining the necessary building materials from various organisations as well as from government supplies (including roof slates, scaffolding and timber). On 23 February 1965, Desmond O'Malley, Parliamentary Secretary to the Minister for Finance, requested the CPW to supply 100 display cases to the KJRS in order for them to be able to mount a proper exhibition in the central hall at the jail.[108]

Opposite, above left: Princess Grace of Monaco was invited to visit the jail by the KJRS.

Opposite, above right: John F. Kennedy – a near visitor in 1963.

Opposite, below: The screen adaptation of Brendan Behan's *The Quare Fellow,* filmed in Kilmainham, 1961/2.

This aerial view of the jail in the early 1960s shows the work of the KJRS in the east wing (to the left) – the roof is almost completely restored. This was an essential aim of the volunteers.

With a very impressive museum collection building up, the committee were still proving very effective at fundraising. As the jail was one of the largest unoccupied jails in Europe, and with a classic Victorian prison design in the east wing, it was no surprise that the committee began to exploit the site's lucrative potential as a film location. In 1962, the screen adaptation of Brendan Behan's play *The Quare Fellow* was filmed in Kilmainham.[109] The jail would be used on many other occasions for such purposes.[110]

10

THE GOLDEN JUBILEE
OF THE 1916 RISING

The remarkably successful work of the KJRS was to culminate in its significant part in the special ceremonies and celebrations held throughout Ireland over Easter 1966 to mark the fiftieth anniversary of the 1916 Rising. The honorary secretary of the KJRS, Piaras Mac Lochlainn, was also secretary of the Coiste Cuimhneachán; the State-funded organising committee for the Golden Jubilee (chaired by the Taoiseach, Seán Lemass and including representatives from many government departments). Many of the KJRS Trustees were also members of the Coiste Cuimhneachán and took an active part in many of the commemorative events.[1] The commemorations were intended to honour those who took part in the Rising and to emphasise its importance as a decisive event in Irish history.

On Easter Sunday, 10 April, the Jubilee events began in earnest, when Dublin, 'was the scene of one of the greatest gatherings in its history as vast crowds packed its main thoroughfares for the commencement of the official commemoration ceremonies'. Approximately 600 veterans of the Rising were present at the occasion, some of whom had come from Britain and the United States. Among the others groups to parade from St Stephen's Green to O'Connell Street were representatives of the Old IRA, the KJRS, national ex-servicemen, and various sporting and cultural organisations. Approximately 2,000 veterans of the War of Independence were also present and included among this group were other members of the KJRS, such as Seán Dowling.

At noon the 1916 Proclamation was read to the crowd by a member of the Defence Forces. The Tricolour was then hoisted with full ceremonial honours on the roof of the GPO. After a salute of twenty-one guns, the military parade began to march past the GPO, where the President, Éamon de Valera, took the salute. Various military units followed different routes, passing most of the buildings in Dublin occupied by the Irish Volunteers in 1916, before converging on O'Connell Street. As the last units in the parade passed the reviewing stand beside the GPO, a flight of Vampire jet aircraft swept overhead. The event concluded with the playing of the National Anthem.

In the afternoon, President de Valera visited Kilmainham Jail and laid a wreath in the yard where the 1916 leaders were executed. Among those present were relatives of the executed leaders, including Roddy Connolly, Nora Connolly O'Brien, Ronan Ceannt, Fr Joseph Mallin and Bridget Colbert.[112] The ceremony was both simple and solemn:

> Following a roll of drums and the presenting of arms, the National flag was lowered to half-mast. Trumpeters sounded the Last Post and honours were rendered by the Special Guard. The President moved forward facing the plaque on the wall of the jail yard, which bears the names of the executed leaders. As he laid the wreath beneath the plaque a roll of drums was sounded, the No. 1 Army Band and the Special Guard rendered honours, and the national flag was hoisted to full mast. Among those attending the ceremony were relatives of the executed leaders and veterans of the Rising and the War of Independence.[113]

The Golden Jubilee parade in Dublin, 1966. Some of the 1916 veterans in the parade were former prisoners in Kilmainham, some were even involved in the restoration.

The 1966 exhibition in the east wing of the jail.

President Éamon de Valera officially launching the new exhibition.

Following the ceremony at the execution plot, the President moved inside to the Kilmainham Jail museum, where he opened the historic exhibition. In the course of his address, de Valera paid tribute to the members of the KJRS, and all those who had worked to bring about the restoration of the jail and its preservation as a historical museum. Recalling the long line of Irish patriots who had spent periods of imprisonment in the jail, the President concluded:

> I do not know of any finer shrine than this old dungeon fortress in which there has been so much suffering and courage so that Ireland should be a nation not only free, but worthy of its great past. This is then a hallowed place and I hope that tens of thousands of our people will come here through the years to visit it and to draw inspiration from it. It is not to continue bitterness that we want to have this place preserved. The reason that we want it is that it will inspire our people and make them remember the great efforts that were made through the centuries to preserve this nation, and encourage them to exalt it among the nations of the earth as the men of 1916 wanted it.[114]

This very significant event in Kilmainham was televised and received extensive coverage in the press and media. The headline in *The Irish Press* the next day was a simple one: 'Kilmainham Becomes a Shrine'.[115] A documentary on the restoration work was screened during Easter week on Raidió Teilifís Éireann.[116] The committee also had an exhibition on the jail at the Royal Dublin Society (RDS) in Ballsbridge at this time. Members of the KJRS attended the various events held through the week, including the official opening of the Garden of Remembrance in Parnell Square. Indeed, coins which were deposited by many people in the central reflecting pool of the garden were later gifted (a not inconsiderable sum in total)[117] to the KJRS. Many members attended the premier of *An Tine Bheo*, a film commissioned from Gael Linn by the Coiste Cuimhneachán, which featured Kilmainham Jail. They attended the launches of special 1916 exhibitions in the National Museum, National Gallery and Municipal Art Gallery. They attended the opening night of *Aiséirí – Glóir-réim na Cásca* (a pageant featuring Irish nationalist history in panorama) at Croke Park, the State Reception at Dublin Castle to mark the Golden Jubilee, ceremonies at Arbour Hill, and many other events.

The KJRS received considerable praise and much excellent exposure throughout the week for their achievements with the restoration work, which was essentially complete. The society had every reason to be proud of their accomplishments. All members of the KJRS were received by President de Valera at a special function in Arás an Uachtaráin after the ceremonies. The Easter week commemorations undoubtedly represented the highpoint of the society. Although the KJRS continued to manage the jail for another twenty years and there would be other highlights, it was never again to equal the excitement of those early years. The restoration work continued, but what the KJRS would have regarded as the essential work was now more or less complete.[118] An exhibition on the Fenians followed in 1967 (the centenary of the Fenian Rising) but although the Taoiseach and other notables attended the launch, it did not attract anything like the same amount of publicity that the 1916 exhibition had the previous year.

The wreath-laying ceremony in the stonebreaker's yard of the jail.

Piaras Mac Lochlainn, secretary of the state-sponsored Coiste Cuimhneachán and secretary of the KJRS, later published *Last Words*, an invaluable collection of last letters and statements of the 1916 leaders.

The re-opening of the Catholic chapel of the jail, October 1971. It was in this chapel that Joseph Plunkett married Grace Gifford just hours before his execution.

By the late 1970s, many of the original members (including Lorcan Leonard, Seán Dowling and James Brennan)[119] had passed away and fundraising became less successful. In 1976, *Cairde Chill Maighneann* (The Friends of Kilmainham) was established by the KJRS in an attempt to provide a permanent reservoir of supporters, but this initiative was unsuccessful. The number of voluntary workers also went into gradual decline – a mere six individuals were offering their services on a regular basis by the mid-1980s. The CPW recently had to spend £10,000 to make one of the jail walls safe.[120] This was on top of the annual subvention of £1,500 a year from the CPW to cover insurance, etc. There were concerns over the danger to documents and artefacts[121] in the collection caused by the damp, dust and lack of adequate supervision, and a number of items were reported missing. There was also some discord between the voluntary workers and the Board of Trustees. The matter was raised in the Dáil by Tomás MacGiolla, who accused the Trustees of treating the jail like their own personal property (no AGMs had been held since the 1970s) and referred to their failure to meet their obligations under the terms of their lease from the government – such as ensuring that the jail was open at all reasonable times.[122] The once inspiring project had seemingly run its course.

Eamon de Valera's last visit to the jail in 1974, aged ninety-two. He died the following year.

Kilmainham Jail – its heroes and songs, an LP brought out by the KJRS in 1979 with contributions from Ronnie Drew, Mary Black and others.

11

UNDER THE CARE OF THE STATE

In 1986, the Board of Trustees, by now considerably diminished in number, handed the upkeep and running of the jail into State care under the Office of Public Works (OPW).[123] As part of the transfer agreement a Board of Visitors was set up. The board was established 'to offer its advice on developments at the jail and conducts annual and other commemorative events associated with Kilmainham'.[124] A supervisor and a curator were appointed at the site by the OPW and employees of the government carried out all maintenance from this point. A £1 million development plan for the jail was announced by the minister for Finance, Ray MacSharry in April 1987.[125] In 1988, the first paid guides were employed in order to expand the opening times. Gradually, the new management brought about many improvements, and overall succeeded in re-energising the old enthusiasm so many had for the jail over the years. Opening times continued to expand and, with the increasing numbers visiting the jail, the tours gradually became necessarily more formal.

Whereas the new guides possibly lacked something of the colour and character of some of the earlier volunteer guides (some of whom had been former prisoners in the jail or close relations of former prisoners), they did provide a generally more reliable service, with vastly improved opening hours. Guides could benefit from an ever-increasing pool of knowledge on the jail, with some guides voluntarily carrying out invaluable research in various archives in Dublin and elsewhere in their free time. The jail has continued to stage numerous events and has been used as a location for extremely popular films, such as *In the Name of the Father* (1993) and *Michael Collins* (1996).[126] Although revenue from film-location fees has yielded profit, the jail remains in existence primarily as an educational resource. This was greatly boosted by the opening, in 1996, of an award-winning museum/interpretive centre, on three levels, climate controlled and constructed within the walls of the jail without damaging any of the historic fabric of the prison. Concepts of imprisonment, the political history associated with the jail (in particular the critical 1916–23 period) and, to a lesser extent, the restoration of the jail, are all treated in the museum. At the same time, a new exhibition on the female political prisoners held in the jail in the 1916–23 period, 'Guns and Chiffon', was launched in the jail. The exhibition would later travel to numerous venues, even as far as New York State.[127]

Beidh fíor chaoin fáilte romhat
chuig oscailt oifigiúil

Éagnairc

Saothar nua ealaíona le

Eoin Mac Lochlainn

I bPríosún Chill Mhaighneann
Bóthar Inse Chór, Baile Átha Cliath 8

Dé Luain, 25ú lá de mhí Aibreáin
ag a 7 a chlog

Urraithe ag
Foras na Gaeilge

Leanfaidh an taispeántas go dtí deireadh mí Meithimh
9.30 – 5.00 i.n., Luan go Domhnach

Éagnairc (Requiem) Art exhibition in the jail by Eoin Mac Lochlainn (son of Piaras Mac Lochlainn) in April 2005.

Numerous exhibitions, often embodying novel interpretive approaches to seeing the jail) have been held in the prison since the early 1990s. Artists from a wide variety of fields (the visual, theatrical, musical and literary arts, prisoners' art,[128] have ever since been consistently drawn to Kilmainham Jail because they wish to situate their artistic statements against the powerful historical or symbolic background of the jail. These events have, almost without exception, been positive for the jail's image, despite many of them being challenging and provocative in nature. In 1991, Kilmainham Jail won a prestigious national arts award for the staging of the 'In a State' art exhibition in the jail. The staging of the Opera Theatre Company's *Emperor of Atlantis* in 2003 received a five-star review from *The London Times*.[129] A 2006, art exhibition by Eoin Mac Lochlainn (son of former KJRS member Piaras Mac Lochlainn) won many positive reviews. All these events have contributed to the prestige of Kilmainham Jail as a major site, not only of historical meaning, but of direct relevance to contemporary cultural life. They have helped draw to Kilmainham many audiences who might otherwise not have visited the site, thus deepening and enhancing its appeal to a wider audience.

But despite these varied explorations, the guide service remains the principal means through which the vast majority of visitors are introduced to its history and meaning – as has been the case since 1960 – with discussion of the 1916 Rising and the Irish nationalist/republican tradition associated with the jail forming a central part of all general tours there.[130]

Above The Italian Job (1969).

Right: The Mackintosh Man (1974).

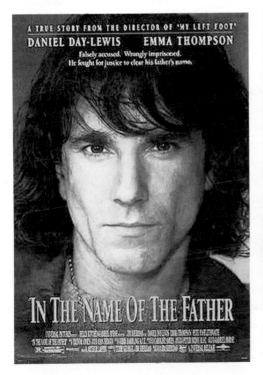

Above: Micheal Collins (1996).

Left: In the Name of the Father (1993).

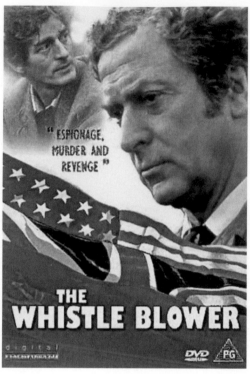

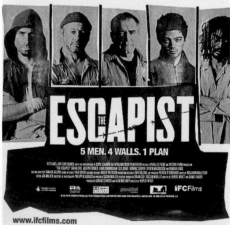

Above left: The Face of Fu Manchu (1965).

Above right: The Whistle Blower (1987).

Left: The Escapist (2008).

12

COMMEMORATION

The type of nationalist/republican commemoration which was continuing in Kilmainham through the 1970s and 1980s was adrift from a general nationwide trend away from such services. State commemoration of the 1916 Rising had been very notably muted since the outbreak of political violence in Northern Ireland in 1969, with much critical and often entirely negative appraisal of the legacy of the Rising by various prominent political commentators. As the Provisional IRA's campaign intensified through the 1970s, members of the liberal intelligentsia and even an Irish government minister (Conor Cruise O'Brien) increasingly denounced the 1916 Rising through guilt by association. In other words, the Provisional IRA were seen as the true heirs to 1916 and any commemoration of the Rising would provide encouragement to that organisation and needlessly provoke unionist reaction. From this viewpoint, the Rising is considered to have been not only undemocratic but also unnecessary and disastrously misguided.

With these views gradually gaining more support in official circles, it was perhaps no surprise that the Diamond Jubilee of the Rising in 1976 witnessed only a very subdued official commemoration, which contrasted sharply with Republican commemorations held throughout the island. As the government disengaged, the initiative was passed to the republicans to claim the sole inheritance of 1916. The sixty-fifth anniversary commemorations in 1981 became a focal point for rallying support for the republican hunger strikers, including Bobby Sands, who was elected MP at this time. The guides and voluntary workers in Kilmainham Jail (a few years before the OPW takeover in 1986) were largely sympathetic to the republican movement (although there had been precious little of such tacit support among the volunteers in the 1960s for the contemporary republican movement).

As republicans continued to dominate 1916 commemorations, the seventy-fifth anniversary of the Rising in 1991 proved a clear example of the reluctance at official level to commemorate the event. This anniversary was too significant a landmark to be ignored. Whatever it symbolised to militant republicans, the Rising remained the historical event most dramatically associated with the Irish struggle for independence and the turning point which lead to its achievement in all but six counties of the island. The Rising had a very significant impact on the ideal of national freedom and it was an event of great emotional power. This 'terrible beauty' could not now be easily left unrecognised or ignored. Yet the *Irish Times* record of the one significant State-sponsored commemorative event seems to speak volumes:

> The Easter Week rebels held out for a week in the GPO but it took only 15 minutes for the State, in the diverse forms of President Robinson and the Taoiseach, Mr Haughey, to commemorate the Rising 75 years later. The Taoiseach had been insisting, of course, that it would be a simple dignified ceremony with no elaborate trimmings and that is what the nation got … The music from the two army bands was the liveliest part of a ceremony which attracted only a few hundred sightseers who clapped politely when it was all over.[131]

A proposal for a commemorative event was made by the curator of Kilmainham Jail, Pat Cooke, who sought to organise a conference on '1916 and its interpretations'. The intention was to provide a forum 'where a whole range of opinions on 1916, and its meanings, could be brought before a wider public'. Some leading historians and commentators on modern Ireland, such as J.J. Lee, Tom Garvin, Declan Kiberd, Gearoid Ó Crualaoich, Michael Laffan, Enda Longley, Arthur Aughley and Seamus Deane, expressed an interest in contributing. As the organisers pointed out, the intention was to provide 'a concert of voices, not a consensus'. However, the conference failed to gain official support and was, again, reluctantly abandoned. Similarly, a great indoor spectacle involving audiovisual presentations, theatre and pageantry, proposed by Professional Event Management (who had actually raised over £100,000 to meet its projected deficit of £150,000 to stage the event) needed an enlightened gesture of £50,000 from the government, but this did not prove forthcoming and the plans had to be abandoned. The government was also disinclined to properly finance the National Museum's attempt to update its 1916 section and the exhibition was inevitably static and outdated, no advance on the exhibition launched in the Golden Jubilee year, twenty-five years before.

Another of those dismayed by the government's grudging acknowledgement of the legacy of 1916 was the artist Robert Ballagh. He headed a group who organised themselves under the banner of 'Reclaim the Spirit of 1916'. A voluntary national organisation, the 75th Anniversary Committee, was established almost one year in advance of the anniversary, in order to attempt to organise a series of events to ensure a fitting commemoration. There were shades here of the early Kilmainham Jail restoration committee.[132] One of the events they organised consisted of poetry, prose and drama readings in Kilmainham Jail. A special dramatic tour, *16-91*, performed by an ensemble of actors and taking the visitors through the events of Easter 1916 through acting and song, attracted remarkable interest through the week. Much disappointment ensued as tours had to be limited, simply to allow the actors to move through the building while performing. It was nonetheless a resounding success. Other events organised by the voluntary 75th Anniversary Committee also achieved some success, most notably an event staged outside the GPO which attracted approximately 10,000 spectators. Conor Cruise O'Brien, and others who shared his outlook on this matter, may not have had any grounds to label official Ireland as 'Provo fellow travellers' (a charge levelled at the 75th committee) but there was still, from the O'Brienite viewpoint, some concern over the many other Irish people who displayed a reluctance, despite the frequently stated dangers, to abandon an old attachment and regard towards the 1916 Rebellion.[133]

The 2nd Eastern Brigade Military Police Company perform a sequence at the wreath-laying ceremony in the stonebreaker's yard, Easter Sunday, 2006.

As the Peace Process gathered strength slowly through the 1990s,[134] it helped introduce a changed atmosphere. In the more optimistic climate, an opportunity was presented to 're-assess the Rising more thoroughly in its own right and with less regard to the identification of the event with the Provisional movement'.[135] A renewed willingness to recognise the importance of the Rising and the Irish nationalist tradition generally (a tradition so powerfully captured in Kilmainham Jail) in official circles became apparent. Early manifestations of this outlook could be seen in the considerable State investment in the 150th anniversary commemorations of the Famine and the bicentenary of the 1798 Rebellion in 1998. A number of State-funded events took place in Kilmainham Jail to commemorate the 1798 Rebellion in particular, with numerous free public lectures from highly regarded academics, an exhibition, a 1798 play, etc. A major exhibition on Robert Emmet in the jail would follow in 2003 (the bicentenary of Emmet's Rebellion). The extent of the changed outlook in official circles, with the Taoiseach Bertie Ahern as seemingly the most enthusiastic advocate, was seen most clearly with the extensive State investment in the commemorations for the ninetieth anniversary of the 1916 Rising in 2006.

Above: Taoiseach Bertie Ahern laying a commemorative wreath in the stonebreaker's yard at Kilmainham Jail, Easter Sunday 2006.

Opposite above: Bertie Ahern with Fr Joseph Mallin, son of Micheal Mallin, who was executed in Kilmainham Jail after the Rising, Easter Sunday 2006.

Opposite below: Pat Rabbitte, Enda Kenny, Bertie Ahern and Mark Durkan talking history at Kilmainham Jail, Easter Sunday 2006.

13

NINETIETH ANNIVERSARY OF THE RISING

The principal day of commemoration, Easter Sunday, 16 April, witnessed a programme of events quite similar to those which took place in 1966 for the Golden Jubilee. A wreath-laying ceremony involving the Taoiseach took place in the stonebreaker's yard in Kilmainham Jail. Following a roll of drums and the presenting of arms, the national flag was lowered to half-mast. Trumpeters sounded the Last Post and honours were rendered by the Special Guard (the 2nd Eastern Brigade Military Police Company). As the Taoiseach laid the wreath beneath the plaque commemorating the executed leaders, a roll of drums was sounded, the Special Guard rendered honours and the national flag was hoisted to full mast. It was the first time such a ceremony had taken place since 1966.

In the Taoiseach's address afterwards, in the east wing of the jail, the 'repositioning' of the official view was crystalline.

Today is about discharging one generation's debt of honour to another. Today, we will fittingly commemorate the patriotism and vision of those who set in train an unstoppable process which led to this country's independence. By gathering here today, 90 years on from the Easter Rising, our presence is testimony to the fact that our generation still cherishes the ideals of the courageous men and women who fought for Ireland in Easter week and during the War of Independence, that we honour and respect their selfless idealism and patriotism, and that we remember with gratitude the great sacrifices they made for us.

Ahern spoke also of his privilege to be in the company of Fr Joseph Mallin, son of one of the executed leaders, Michael Mallin; the only surviving child of any of the 1916 leaders, who had travelled from Hong Kong. The elderly priest, aged ninety-two, had visited his father in Kilmainham Jail shortly before his execution.[136] He had also attended the wreath-laying ceremony in Kilmainham in 1966.

At noon, preparations for a military parade[137] from Dublin Castle to Parnell Square were complete, with an estimated 120,000 spectators gathered to witness the event. As in 1966, there was a large reviewing stand erected outside the GPO, with government ministers present, ministers of state, council of state members, diplomatic corps, the Lord Mayor and the Taoiseach. On arrival, the President, Mary McAleese, inspected the Guard of Honour, the national flag was lowered, the 1916 Proclamation was read by an army officer, and the President laid a wreath. This was followed by a minute's silence for those who died. The national flag was then raised to full mast and the national anthem was played. The parade then got under way. There was general agreement that the whole event was dignified and moving and that the organisation had been first class.

With a number of important documentaries relating to the Rising being filmed in the jail (including a film on the Rising) and an acclaimed play, *Operation Easter*, written by Donal Kelly and performed in the east wing of the jail, the anniversary year saw public awareness and interest in Kilmainham increasing yet more. Ever since, visitor numbers continue to rise: in 2008 there were over 299,563 visitors to the jail, the highest number yet recorded.[138] Since 2006, a regular journal, *Sentences*, has been produced by staff working at the jail, consisting of research articles by various members of staff. This journal is of great value to anyone studying the history of Kilmainham and continues to extend the corpus of knowledge on the jail. This is very much in keeping with the ideals of the restoration committee in the early years. The future appears to be secured and in many respects the hopes of the original KJRS have now been truly realised.

Patricia Reynolds Byrne (centre), granddaughter of former Fenian prisoner Jeremiah O'Donovan Rossa, visiting Kilmainham jail with her family in 2007. Patricia was just one of many descendents of former prisoners who have visited in recent years.

14

CONCLUSION

Overall, the story of the Kilmainham Jail since 1924 has been quite remarkable. Seán Fitzpatrick of the National Graves Association deserves the credit for initiating the whole idea of developing the jail as a national monument. His suggestions to the early Fianna Fáil government had a very sound and reasonable basis. The two open days at the jail in 1938 proved there was very significant public interest. Fianna Fáil could have easily exploited the site for its own interests. Indeed, with so many of the party having connections with the jail, most famously de Valera (under death sentence in Kilmainham in 1916 and the last prisoner held in the jail at the end of the Civil War), it is difficult to understand why there was so much procrastination on their part. De Valera is renowned for his skilful use of symbol, yet this appears to be one of the occasions where this ability failed him.

Though many discussed the potential of the jail over the years, it was Lorcan Leonard who was to show the imagination as well as the practical wherewithal to really begin to conceptualise exactly how to go about the undertaking. Leonard was aided by many notable individuals, such as P.J. Stephenson and Seamus Brennan. Leonard was also considerably assisted by Seán Dowling (who became the first Chairman of the KJRS) and the Old IRA Association – whose members were very prominent in the early years of the restoration committee.

The committee successfully captured the popular imagination and the spirit and enthusiasm of the early volunteers was particularly noteworthy. Their work represented a unique example of what they perceived as practical patriotism and, in many ways, marked the end of an era. The new Ireland emerging at this time, although confident and forward looking, would certainly not be noted for its voluntary ethos or any real culture of active citizenship. Bearing in mind that the work at Kilmainham was all voluntary, the considerable administrative work undertaken by Leonard, Piaras Mac Lochlainn and others, the courtesy shown to so many visitors to the jail, and the hard physical and skilled labour undertaken by the other volunteers, is all the more striking.

Interestingly, it was the Fianna Fáil party who gained all the political capital from the jail. On their numerous visits to the jail, Lemass and de Valera always appeared to have been intimately connected with the restoration and this perhaps helps to explain why the Labour Party, in 1966, jealously accused the committee of being a Fianna Fáil organisation.[139] In fact, the committee was a disparate group from many different backgrounds, some with no interest at all in contemporary politics.[140] All were, however, agreed on the notion of preserving the jail as a monument to 'Ireland's heroic dead'. That tradition continues to be respected, although, as has been seen, the jail is now more open to different interpretations through various mediums.

Perhaps the last word should be left to Lorcan Leonard, who made Seán Fitzpatrick's vision a reality. In a letter written shortly before his death in 1965, as preparations were being made for the opening of a museum in the jail the following year, Leonard concluded his letter in a manner that encapsulates the reverential impulse and patriotic spirit that inspired the whole restoration endeavour:

> I am convinced as I always was … out of our poor efforts at least the children of the future will say we preserved the history of Ireland, as far as stone and roofs are concerned, for Kilmainham is the Calvary of republicanism in Ireland. Let them say we gave them neither wealth nor land, but a dream.

Cross in the stonebreaker's yard of the jail where the 1916 leaders were executed.

APPENDIX 1

A SELECTION OF NOTABLE POLITICAL PRISONERS HELD IN KILMAINHAM JAIL

Kilmainham Jail opened as the county jail for Dublin in August 1796. Within a month, the prison began to receive its first state or political prisoners, members of the Society of United Irishmen which had been declared an illegal organisation.

NOTABLE UNITED IRISHMEN HELD IN THE JAIL AT VARIOUS TIMES, 1796-1799

Samuel Neilson

Henry Joy McCracken (hanged in Belfast, 17 July 1798)

Oliver Bond

William J. MacNeven (exiled to Fort George, Scotland in March 1799)

Thomas Addis Emmet (exiled to Fort George, Scotland in March 1799)

Edward Hudson (exiled to Fort George, Scotland in March 1799)

John Sweetman (exiled to Fort George, Scotland in March 1799)

John Sheares (hanged in Dublin, 14 July 1798)

Henry Sheares (hanged in Dublin, 14 July 1798)

James Napper Tandy

1803

Robert Emmet (hanged in Dublin, 19 September 1803)

Thomas Russell (hanged in Downpatrick, October 1803)

Anne Devlin

Michael Dwyer (transported to New South Wales, July 1805)

St John Mason (author of *Prison Abuses in Ireland*, 1810)

1848: YOUNG IRELANDERS

Thomas Francis Meagher (transported to Van Dieman's Land, July 1849)

William Smith O'Brien (transported to Van Dieman's Land, July 1849)

Patrick O'Donohoe (transported to Van Dieman's Land, July 1849)

1865-7: FENIANS

John O'Leary

Charles Kickham

Jeremiah O'Donovan Rossa

Thomas Clarke Luby

Charles Underwood O'Connell

Dennis Dowling Mulcahy

Daniel Byrne

Stephen Joseph Meany

Major John A. Comerford (served in the Union army in the American Civil War)

General William Halpin (served in the Union army in the American Civil War)

General Thomas Francis Burke (served in the Confederate army in the Civil War)

Colonel John Warren

Captain Augustine Costelloe

1880S: LAND LEAGUE LEADERS

Michael Davitt

Charles Stewart Parnell

John Dillon

Tim Healy

William O'Brien

Thomas Sexton

Thomas Brennan

A.J. Kettle

Fr Eugene Sheehy

Josephe Walshe

1883: 'THE INVINCIBLES'

Joseph Brady (hanged in Kilmainham Jail, 9 June 1883)

Daniel Curley (hanged in Kilmainham Jail, 9 June 1883)

Timothy Kelly (hanged in Kilmainham Jail, 9 June 1883)

Michael Fagan (hanged in Kilmainham Jail, 9 June 1883)

Thomas Caffrey (hanged in Kilmainham Jail, 9 June 1883)

1908

Laurence Ginnell (nationalist MP, wrote *Land and Liberty* in the jail)

1916

Patrick Pearse (executed in Kilmainham Jail, 3 May 1916)

Thomas Clarke (executed in Kilmainham Jail, 3 May 1916)

Thomas MacDonagh (executed in Kilmainham Jail, 3 May 1916)

Joseph Mary Plunkett (executed in Kilmainham Jail, 4 May 1916)

William Pearse (executed in Kilmainham Jail, 4 May 1916)

Michael O'Hanrahan (executed in Kilmainham Jail, 4 May 1916)

Edward Daly (executed in Kilmainham Jail, 4 May 1916)

John MacBride (executed in Kilmainham Jail, 5 May 1916)

Seán Heuston (executed in Kilmainham Jail, 8 May 1916)

Éamonn Ceannt (executed in Kilmainham Jail, 8 May 1916)

Michael Mallin (executed in Kilmainham Jail, 8 May 1916)

Con Colbert (executed in Kilmainham Jail, 8 May 1916)

James Connolly (executed in Kilmainham Jail, 12 May 1916)

Seán MacDiarmada (executed in Kilmainham Jail, 12 May 1916)

Numerous other notable figures were held in Kilmainham under sentence of death only to have their sentences commuted. The Countess Markievicz was the only women who had to endure this predicament. Other notable female political prisoners in the jail at the time included Kathleen Lynn, Countess Plunkett, Madeleine Ffrench-Mullen, Nellie Gifford and Winnie Carney.

1920-21: WAR OF INDEPENDENCE

Rory O'Connor

Oscar Traynor

Ernie O'Malley

Frank Teeling

Simon Donnelly

Fr Dominic

Frank Flood (later transferred to Mountjoy Jail and hanged 14 March 1921)

Bernard Ryan (later transferred to Mountjoy Jail and hanged 14 March 1921)

Patrick Doyle (later transferred to Mountjoy Jail and hanged 14 March 1921)

Thomas Bryan (later transferred to Mountjoy Jail and hanged 14 March 1921)

Thomas Whelan (later transferred to Mountjoy Jail and hanged 14 March 1921)

Patrick Moran (later transferred to Mountjoy Jail and hanged 14 March 1921)

1922-24: CIVIL WAR

Female prisoners:

Maud Gonne MacBride

Mary MacSwiney

Margaret Buckley

Dorothy Macardle

Grace Plunkett

Sighle Humphreys

Kathleen Clarke

Male prisoners:

Dan Breen

Tom Barry

Peter Cassidy (executed in Kilmainham Jail, 17 November 1922)

James Fisher (executed in Kilmainham Jail, 17 November 1922)

John Gaffney (executed in Kilmainham Jail, 17 November 1922)

Richard Twohig   (executed in Kilmainham Jail, 17 November 1922)

Terence Brady (executed in Portobello Barracks, 8 January 1923)

Leo Dowling (executed in Portobello Barracks, 8 January 1923)

Sylvester Heaney (executed in Portobello Barracks, 8 January 1923)

Anthony O'Reilly (executed in Portobello Barracks, 8 January 1923)

Laurence Sheehy (executed in Portobello Barracks, 8 January 1923)

Peadar O'Donnell

Frank Gallagher

Andrew McDonnell (later an important figure in the restoration of the jail)

Ernie O'Malley

Tomás Derrig

Gerard Boland

Seán T. O'Kelly

Austin Stack

Éamon de Valera (the last prisoner held in Kilmainham Jail)

APPENDIX 2

LETTER SENT BY SEÁN FITZPATRICK TO DUBLIN COUNTY COUNCIL, 20 MAY, 1931

P.J. Murphy, Esq.,
Secretary,
County Council,
11 Parnell Square,
Dublin,

A Chara,

Some time ago when the writer and members of his Committee had the privilege of visiting Kilmainham prison, we were grieved to perceive the very considerable, and to our mind deliberate, damage done to the building, and the dirty and neglected condition in which the entire place was.

To Irish Nationalists, Kilmainham holds many dear associations, and is a veritable shrine of national sacrifice. For close on a century the place was the Calvary of Ireland, and it was with a feeling of reverence that we approached the place, but what a shock we got!

Since our visit it has been reported to us that it is the intention of your Council to take the necessary steps to preserve the place from further destruction, and, we hope, to preserve the very fine paintings and drawings executed by the many occupants from time to time. I am sure very little research would be necessary to locate the cells occupied by the many imprisoned there for loving and serving their country as God gave them the light to do.

The Cardinal point of consideration to our Committee is the marking and preservation of the graves of Irish Patriots buried within the prison and the necessary work to enshrine that spot on which so much of the best blood of Ireland freely flowed at dawn on the May mornings of 1916.

We were sorry to find the place in such a condition on our visit, but we are certain that it is merely necessary to draw your attention and that of your elected Council to this matter to have it attended to, as Kilmainham is one of the places that many of our exiled brethren will visit during their stay in Dublin for the Eucharistic Congress next year.

An early reply as to what is proposed by your Council as regards the buildings and Graves would be greatly favoured.

Yours faithfully,
Honorary Secretary
National Graves Association

APPENDIX 3

PROPOSAL

1 JANUARY 1960

OUTLINE PROPOSALS FOR THE RESTORATION OF KILMAINHAM JAIL

Considered and approved by the Kilmainham Jail Restoration Committee

Preamble

It is understood that the government are considering a scheme for the restoration of Kilmainham Jail but we fear that having regard for the commitments of the Department of Finance, the scheme at best is of modest dimensions, and we believe that a larger scale plan is required.

Having inspected the site with our technical advisors, we are most concerned with the condition of the building, and are very conscious of the urgent need of an early effort to arrest the decay by at least making the whole structure weatherproof.

It is possible that when the time comes to proceed with the government's proposals, the appropriate government department may well be advised by the Commissioners of Public Works that the task, if not impossible, is uneconomic. We do not wish to appear critical of the Commissioners of Public Works in this matter, but being conscious of the place that Kilmainham occupies in our history, and of the hopes and dreams of those who were incarcerated there, and conscious of the national demand for the preservation of Kilmainham, we submit the following scheme for your consideration.

If Kilmainham Jail could be taken over by a Board of Trustees who themselves are sufficiently conscious of the need to preserve it, and to organise the restoration of the jail to an Historical Museum it would constitute a major step forward in civilian initiative and would be of immeasurable value to future generations, not to mention the immediate asset of a tourist attraction.

When the committee has accomplished the task of restoration, then the site could be finally handed over to such Trustees forever. On the other hand if the project falls short of the target, then after the period of five years, the property can revert back to the Commissioners of Public Works.

The scheme, as outlined hereafter, based on the idea of voluntary labour, is one which has been considered for the project and accepted by the committee, as practical and which, if undertaken, and completed, would demonstrate the potentialities of voluntary effort, which at the moment is almost untapped for such enterprises. The scheme could also relieve the National Exchequer of a considerable burden.

Board of Trustees

A Board of Trustees would be agreed upon and would consist of persons of integrity and public standing, willing to act as Trustees.

It is expected that such people are in themselves physically and/or mentally related to all that Kilmainham represents in the courage and hope and thought of the Irish nation. The actual operation of the scheme will not necessarily fall on the shoulders of the Board of Trustees, but a committee of management would be formed who would in turn be responsible to the Board of Trustees and who would undertake the actual work.

Committee of Management

The Committee of Management would be formed of people who are willing and able to undertake such a task and would preferably and only be persons who have knowledge of building construction and have general management ability. The Committee would be essentially in two parts, and when acting separately would automatically form two subcommittees, namely the building subcommittee and the finance subcommittee. Under these two subcommittees would be tracked all the various task forces essential to the restoration of Kilmainham.

Name of the Organisation

The project will be given the name of 'Kilmainham Restoration'.

Objects

The principal would be the complete restoration of Kilmainham Jail and the establishment of a Historical Museum and the enshrinement of the area in which the leaders of the 1916 Rising were executed. In addition, it is visualised that the complete area containing Kilmainham Jail borders on the east by the South Circular Road, on the north of Inchicore Road, on the west by Grattan Crescent, and on the south by Emmet Road, be converted into a Garden of Remembrance and would be open to the public.

The complete site is excellently situated for such a park, with a gentle southern slope to the Camac River which bisects the site for its entire length. With the proper planning and

Treatment of the river, together with good landscaping, this area could be turned into a showpiece of the city besides providing amenities to the people of the Inchicore area.

Conditions of Acceptance of Building site

The wall and all the lands relating thereto would have to be handed over free of rent and rates for ever to the Board of Trustees, and as the leases run out of the property in the area described under 'objects' it is visualised that all such sites should be handed over to the Board of Trustees, and again free of rent and rates for ever.

Financing of Project

The task of restoration and the future development would be undertaken by voluntary labour and the materials required contributed by others or purchased with funds received by the Finance Committee. All the work on the site would be voluntary labour operating after normal working hours or on normal days of rest. The voluntary labour is forthcoming and will provide another dimension to the project and thus in itself attract to the organisation the best of our citizens.

Immediate Task of Building Subcommittee

The first task of the building subcommittee, after possession of the site has been obtained, is to have a complete and detailed survey of the buildings and services, carried out by an Architect in consultation with a Civil Engineer and a Mechanical and Electrical Engineer. Architect: Dermot O'Toole, Civil Engineer: Fergus Clarke, Mechanical and Electrical Engineer: L. Leonard. This team under the general control of the Architect would prepare three programmes for submission to the Management Committee:

1. Immediate stabilisation of the existing buildings, and to prevent further deterioration.
2. Plan of Restoration of Kilmainham Jail.
3. Plans of future site development.

The Construction Team

There will be a minimum labour force of the following – 2 Storekeepers, 6 Bricklayers and Masons, 4 Plasterers, 4 Carpenters, 4 Slaters, 4 Painters, 30 Labourers, 2 Fitters, 3 Plumbers, 3 Electricians, 6 Helpers or Apprentices.

This labour can be readily recruited and at the moment the present minimum requirements can be met from those who have already been approached for their services. No payment of any kind will be expected and their services are offered voluntarily.

However provision will be made for the following incidentals to this construction task force. Insurance (personal injuries), Canteen, Washroom, and cloakroom facilities: the provision of these services should be one of the duties of the Finance subcommittee.

Finance subcommittee for immediate future

This committee would be complimentary to and in support of the Building subcommittee and would have the following tasks and staff:

1. Provision of General office staff, typists, accountants, caretaker, etc.
2. Provision of Canteen and staff necessities.
3. Raising of funds by (a) Questing for materials required by construction team (b) Organising subscriptions from different sources and individuals (c) Questing for suppliers to staff canteen (d) Publicity Department, including lectures, willing to address all social organisations.

Time and Cost

The restoration of the jail and conversion to a museum would take approximately four to five years, and the probable cost of the materials (if purchased) assuming always that all labour is voluntary; the figure will be £60–70,000.

(*Source*: Department of the Taoiseach files, S. 6521 D/63, 2 March 1960.)

APPENDIX 4

LETTER OF ACCEPTANCE FROM DEPARTMENT OF FINANCE

2 Marta 1960

A Chara,

I am directed by the Minister for Finance to inform you that the government have agreed to allow your Committee to proceed with your proposals for the restoration of Kilmainham Jail, subject to the following conditions:

1. The property will be leased, in accordance with section 10 of the State Property Act 1954 to Trustees, two of whom will be nominated by the Minister, for a term of five years at a nominal rent of 1d a year, if demanded, the state to indemnify the Trustees against the payment of any rates which may be assessable on the property.

2. If the committee of management fail to implement the scheme or to make satisfactory progress, the property will revert to the Commissioners of PW.

3. The Committee will submit to the Minister, for prior approval, the plans or detailed proposals for reconstruction – if necessary in stages.

4. Subject to satisfactory progress, the property on completion of the restoration will be transferred to the Trustees by way of grant or on a long-term lease in accordance with section 10 of the State Property Act, the Deed of Grant or Lease will impose upon the Trustees the responsibility for the management and maintenance of the property. Power can be taken for the filling of vacancies among the Trustees as occasion arises.

Subject to your Committee accepting these conditions, the Minister proposes to issue, through the government information bureau, a statement on the lines of the attached draft on which your Committee may wish to comment. I am to request that the matter be treated as confidential pending the issue of the statement from the government information bureau.

Mise, Le Meas
(Document unsigned)

(*Source*: Letter from Department of Finance to the KJRC, 2 March 1960, Department of the Taoiseach Files, S. 6521 D/63.)

APPENDIX 5

CONSTITUTION AND RULES OF THE KILMAINHAM JAIL RESTORATION SOCIETY

1. The Kilmainham Jail Restoration Society was registered as a limited liability company in the year 1961 and the regulations set out in the Memorandum and Articles of Association shall continue to be the rules of the Society with the following additional or amended rules adopted by the Council of the Society at a meeting on 7 December 1962.

2. The Council of the Society shall be empowered at any time to make such rule or rules which may seem to them to be necessary for the proper conduct of the Society and any rule so made by the council shall be binding on members of the Society until the next Annual General Meeting of the Society for ratification, amendment, or rejection.

3. The aims of the society shall be:
(a) To restore and acquire Kilmainham Jail and to preserve and maintain it as a monument to the patriots who were imprisoned there.
(b) To establish in the jail a National Museum.
(c) To promote and encourage study of history and archaeology and in particular the history and archaeology of the jail and its occupants.
(d) To make arrangement for the acquisition, collection, preservation and exhibition of prints, books and documents, records and assets and property of every description having an historical interest or value particularly in relation to the jail.
(e) To arrange lectures and discussions on matters of historical interest, and to arrange for the printing and publication of lectures and articles, and the dissemination of knowledge in relation to persons.
(f) To provide and maintain Meeting Rooms, Reading Rooms, Library, Museum and Exhibition Rooms and such other conveniences in connection therewith as may be considered necessary or desirable to promote the objects of the Society and the exchange of information and social intercourse between members.
(g) To construct, maintain, and alter any houses, buildings, or works necessary or convenient for the purpose of the Society.

(h) To take any gift of property, whether subject to any Trust or not, for any one or more of the objects of the Society.

(i) To take such steps by personal or written appeals, public meetings or otherwise as may from time to time be deemed expedient for the purpose of procuring contributions to the funds of the Society in the shape of donations, annual subscriptions or otherwise.

(j) To print any newspapers, periodicals, books leaflets or reports that the Society may think desirable for the promotion of its objects.

(k) To sell, manage, lease, mortgage, dispose of, or otherwise deal with all or any part of the property of the Society.

(l) To borrow and raise money as the Society may think fit.

(m) To invest any monies of the Society not immediately required for any of its objects, in such manner as may from time to time be determined on.

(n) To undertake and execute any trusts which may seem directly or indirectly conducive to any of the objects of the Society.

(o) To do all such other lawful things as are incidental or conducive to the attainment of the above objects.

4. Membership. The ordinary Members of the Society shall be:

(a) The Trustees of Kilmainham Jail

(b) The Members of the Committee of Management for the time being as approved by the Trustees.

(c) The members of the Committees working on the restoration project under the direction of the Committee of Management as follows: the Site Committee, the Publicity Committee, the Finance Committee, the Museum and Historical Committee, the Guided Committee and the Canteen Committee.

(d) Voluntary workers on the Restoration Project nominated by the site Committee.

(e) Subscriptions of 25 or more to the Restoration Project subject to the approval of the council.

5. Associate Members may be admitted to the Society at the discretion of the Council and shall be required to pay an annual subscription of two guineas. Associate Members shall not be eligible to vote at meetings of the Society but shall be entitled to all other rights and privileges of Ordinary Members.

6. (a) Honorary Members may be admitted to the Society at the discretion of the Council. Honorary Members shall not enjoy all the rights and privileges of Associate Members but shall not be required to pay any annual subscription or any entrance fee.

(b) An Honorary Member shall be one who, in the opinion of the Council, has rendered national service to Ireland or who has contributed to the renown of Ireland by his literary, historical, or artistic work.

7. Council

(a) The Council shall consist of Honorary Officers and twelve Ordinary Members.

(b) The Honorary Officers shall be the President, one or two Vice-Presidents, one or two Honorary Secretaries, the Honorary Treasurer, the Honorary Editor and other such Honorary Officers as may from time to time be determined by the Society.

(c) At the Annual General Meeting in each year the Society shall elect a President and other Honorary Officers (except the Honorary Editor) to fill the places of those retiring. The Honorary Officers so elected shall hold office until the next Annual General Meeting when they shall retire but be eligible for re-election.

(d) Of the twelve Ordinary Members of the Council five shall be elected at the Annual General Meeting. The remaining seven shall be nominated by the Site Committee.

(e) The seven members to be nominated by the Site Committee shall be elected at the general meeting of the voluntary workers on the Restoration Project convened for that purpose by the Site Committee at least seven days before the Annual General Meeting of the Society.

(f) The Council shall at its first meeting in each year to be held after the Annual General Meeting of the Society elect the Honorary Editor who shall hold office until the election meeting in the following year when he shall retire, but be eligible for re-election. The Honorary Editor shall *virtute officio* be a member of the Council but the Council shall have the power at any time to remove an Hon. Editor and to appoint another member in his place who shall hold office until the next election meeting and shall be eligible for re-election

(g) Casual vacancies among the Hon. Officers or ordinary members of the Council may be fulfilled by the Council by co-opting a member to fill the vacancy, but the person so co-opted shall retire at the next Annual General Meeting when he shall be eligible for re-election.

(h) The Office of the Honorary Officer or of the ordinary member of the Council shall be vacated:

    (I) If he shall die or resign.

    (II) If he shall cease to be a member of the Society.

    (III) If he shall be absent from meetings of the Council for a period of six months without having leave of absence from the Council.

    (IV) If he shall be convicted of an indictable offence.

    (V) If he shall become a bankrupt or of unsound mind.

(i) The quorum of a meeting of the Council shall be four, unless otherwise determined by the Council, and no meeting shall be transacted at a meeting of the Council or the Society unless a quorum is present. At least fourteen days notice shall be given in writing to each member of the Society of the date and place of the Annual General Meeting in each year.

(*Source*: Restoration Documents file, Kilmainham Jail Archives Collection, n/d.)

APPENDIX 6

KILMAINHAM RESTORATION PROJECT

[Issued by the Site Committee in 1960]

TO ALL MEMBERS OF THE LABOUR TASK FORCE:

As work proceeds, certain organisational difficulties arise, especially in regard to the authority each member of the Task Force should have and also to the behaviour and discipline expected of each member of that Force.

It has been decided by the Site Committee, the names of whom appear below, that this circular will be handed to each and every member of the Task Force so that all shall be familiar with procedure.

The responsibility for the planning, reconstruction, and delegation of labour, and safety of personnel, within the Jail, rests solely with the Site Committee and all members of the Labour Task Force on entering the Jail will be subject to the instruction of the Committee and the discipline they decide is necessary to assist the task of Restoration and the safety of those engaged on the work.

Realising always, that the effort is voluntary, as all efforts in the past history of Irish Republicans was voluntary, it is expected that each and every member of the Task Force will apply sufficient self-discipline worthy of the task undertaken and the ground on which the work takes place.

It is desirable that each member of the Task Force should be attached to a group to which a certain task has been allotted and when reporting for duty, will proceed to that task without further direction. From time to time, it may be necessary at the discretion of the Committee, to re-allocate personnel to different duties, depending on the weather and the numbers on duty at any given time. At all times, each member of the Task Force should be prepared to undertake any task allotted to him.

No members of the Labour Task Force are permitted to bring visitors to the Jail, without the consent of at least one member of the Committee and no visitors are permitted to take photographs or carry cameras, without written authorisation of the Committee.

At no time shall any member of the Labour Task Force act as a guide for visitors to the Jail, unless specifically requested to do so, by a member of the Site Committee and if delegated to act as a guide, on no account must any gratuity be accepted from visitors.

As stated above, all members of the Labour Task Force are under the control of the Site Committee, and any complaints, irregularities, or indiscipline must be reported to the Committee, who will decide the action to be taken after granting an opportunity to the persons concerned to appear before the Site Committee.

Any gifts of cigarettes, etc., from the Canteen, depends entirely on manufacturers donating same to the Canteen, and no guarantee is given that such supplies has been or will be maintained.

Please remember at all times, that each and every member is privileged by being identified with the Labour Task Force in one of the grandest efforts made to honour and perpetuate the memory of our illustrious dead.

Enter the Jail then as you would a shrine.

Conduct yourself there as you would in a house of prayer.

Leave it a better man than when you came in.

ISSUED BY THE SITE COMMITTEE
Lorcan Leonard (Chairman)
Harry White (Secretary)
Pat Early, Paddy Kelly, George Tully, Dinny Duggan, Joe Collins, Charlie Gorman, Paddy Brown, Jim Bruce, Denis Walsh, Seán O'Ruairc, Pat Bannon

APPENDIX 7

'THE KILMAINHAM PROJECT AS I DREAMT IT AND LIVED IT' BY LORCAN LEONARD

CHAPTER 1: THE BEGINNING

'At sometime, at some place, and by some one must a start be made'.
Fintan Lalor

Being a Northsider, and as a child, south of the River Liffey was considered Indian territory, not to be visited unless accompanied by stout companions. The result was that I knew very little about the south side in contrast to the detailed knowledge I had of buildings, back streets, lanes and holes in walls on the north side. One knew of the City Hall, the Castle, the Coombe, the Liberties, etc., but these were very far away places surrounded by 'southsiders'.

It was not until I was married and had rented a house on the Naas Road that I took a serious interest in the buildings of the south side, and in particular Kilmainham Jail, since I was living close enough to it. It was 1942.

One day while awaiting a bus at the intersection of Emmet Road and the South Circular Road, I fell to contemplating the old jail, which was citadelled before me on the rising ground. Never before had I noted the perfect stone work in the central compound which arose high over the forbidding boundary walls. Somehow there was friendliness there in Kilmainham. Perhaps it was the knowledge of those who, for one hundred and fifty years had passed through it to their deaths at home and abroad, that gave it an indefinable sense of warmth and security. My bus eventually came along and I went my way never to think actively again on Kilmainham until 1952. In that year, myself and Tommy O'Brien were discussing the Invincibles and the fact that these men were completely ignored by succeeding generations. Even radical republican thought, for what that was worth, maintained an ignorance of them. Evidently the efforts of the Invincibles were too 'earthy' for even their refined palates. We agreed that we would try, even in a modest way, to do something that would perpetrate their memory.

We decided to make a documentary film on the Invincibles and utilise any money obtained through the showing of the film to put a memorial in Kilmainham Jail or some other suitable site. We enlisted the help of 'Cre' O'Farrell who at the time had, as a hobby, shot some good films on several subjects. I then endeavoured to enlist further help and I approached John Dowling and Paddy Stephenson.

The former advised me that I was dealing with a dangerous subject which was best left alone and at any rate no help would be forthcoming from him, and the latter said that he could not be identified with the project, but he agreed with the proposals and would give me any information or pursue any research on the Invincibles that I thought necessary for the film.

Having deliberated on the reactions of Dowling and Paddy Stephenson, we decided to go ahead just the three of us and to hell with 'well-known names'.

The project got 'bogged down' when we found that the gates of Kilmainham were closed to us as far as taking any shots inside the jail was concerned. The enthusiasm died and nothing further was done.

When the Technical School at Emmet Road was being built, I met up with the Clerk-of-Works on this job, Bob Payne, and often talked to him regarding the disgraceful way that Kilmainham was neglected. We could see the old jail through the window of his office, and one day he informed me that he had on good authority that the Office of Public Works would shortly invite tenders for the demolition of the jail. This was indeed bad news to me, this was indeed the last act of the Philistines who had already provided a rash of 'Mother Éires' and Celtic crosses from one end of the country to the other to prove I suppose, the respectable and Catholic character of the 'Four Glorious' years.

I met Paddy Stephenson one night at a meeting of the Old Dublin Society and during the course of a few drinks after the meeting I got the promise of his support for any action I might take or organise short of 'mass action' to preserve the jail. He said that within a few years he would be out on pension and then he wouldn't give a damn what action was taken.

Paddy and I discussed this matter time and time again and when on holidays at Lisdoonvarna in the summer of 1958, I made a draft of a plan of restoration based on voluntary labour and to turn the jail into a historical museum.

On my return to Dublin, Paddy was delighted, and after some minor adjustments to the plan it was decided to call a meeting of some people who would be interested and who by their 'records' would add weight to our eventual petition to the government.

I booked a room in Jury's Hotel in September 1958 and amongst those who attended on invitation were Jimmy Brennan, Stephen Murphy, John Dowling and some others.

Paddy Stephenson read out my proposals for the restoration of the jail and after much discussion the general view was sceptical because it could not be believed that voluntary labour could be obtained for such a project. However, it was agreed to pursue the matter further.

The only persons who did 'pursue the matter further' were Jimmy Brennan, Stephen Murphy, myself and Paddy Stephenson. Paddy acted chairman at all meetings. Sometimes Dan Stephenson turned up at the request of his father but his contributions were little or nothing.

In view of his later contribution to Kilmainham, it is well to state that John Dowling never put in an appearance during those early meetings of what we called the Provisional Committee.

It was agreed at these meetings that in order to preserve unity of purpose nothing relating to events after 1921 would be introduced into any activity, publicity or statements in connection with Kilmainham.

I undertook to raise the necessary volunteer labour force and Harry White, Paddy Gannon and myself circularised upwards of one hundred and fifty men known to us as republicans, and who at one time or another were closely identified with the Republican Movement. It was felt that out of this group would come the core of the voluntary effort, since the men circularised needed no instruction on Kilmainham or its unique position, as a building, in the republican history of Ireland. A copy of the circular is appended.

At the same time, I think 200 circulars were sent out to people by the Provisional Committee asking them to allow their names to be quoted as supporting the proposals in the petition to the Government.
I think we got about forty favourable replies and one or two unfavourable ones.

We also got an interview with the Congress of Irish Union and myself and Paddy Stephenson had their assurances that they would in no way frown on such a voluntary effort and while they could not publicly support it, privately they were glad that an effort was being made to restore the jail to a museum.

Subsequently the Building Trades Council stated that they had no objection to the recruitment of voluntary labour for such an enterprise. Two meetings were held in the pre-Truce IRA rooms in Pearse Street for the voluntary labour task force and the plans for restoration were detailed to the men. The attendance at these two meetings was disappointingly small, but it was agreed that if and when the jail was handed over to the committee enough men could be recruited.

I, on both occasions assured the men, as I was assured by the committee, at least those members who were consistently attending meetings, made an inspection of the site and with us came Dermot O'Toole and Fergus Clarke who I had recruited to give the committee any architectural or structural advice when desired.

The condition inside the jail defied description and an extract from a report I read before a public meeting in the Mansion House is indicative of the jungle that existed there.

Access could be obtained to the stonebreaker's yard (1916 execution yard) through the paved court and along the paved area down to the south-west corner of the site where the Invincibles are buried. From this point along the south end of the site all the exercise yards were impassable as also was the open area running along the east wall leading to the infirmary. The inner yards at the governor's quarters and the infirmary and also the path joining the Infirmary to the inner foyer of the jail entrance were completely blocked.

When I say the yards or paths were impassable or blocked I am not exaggerating, the whole open areas to the south, east and north was a jungle. Trees standing 20 to 30 feet high with a dense undergrowth of brambles and thorn bushes from four to five feet high. The condition of the inner yard of the '98 section of the prison defies description. The external walls of the site running from 30 to 40 feet high were festooned with ivy especially along the north, east and south sides, so much so that the actual walls could not be seen.

The section of the jail fronting on the Inchicore Road consists of the administration wing, governor's apartments and the infirmary. Of these buildings only the west section of the administration wing and the infirmary had roofs and floors in relatively good condition, but all doors, windows and fireplaces had been removed. The centre section of the administration wing and the governor's apartments were in a ruinous condition with the roofs ready to fall and the intermediate floors hanging crazily from the butt ends of the flooring joists still caught in the walls. Only the walls had successfully withstood the onslaught of the elements.

The jail proper consists of an inner court surrounded by buildings. This is an early section built in the 1790s and a central compound built in the 1850s. There are three tiers of cells along the sides and a large open area 40 feet wide and 110 feet long by 60 feet high in the centre.

The roofs to the north and south wings of the '98 section of the jail were in a very poor condition but could still be saved. The roofs to the west and east wings had completely collapsed except in some places, where the old roof trusses could not find enough space to fall into. The intermediate floors with cells along the north, west and south wings, were intact because of the vaulted ceilings and flagged floors in these wings. However, the east wing which contained the Church of Ireland chapel and the Catholic chapel together with condemned cells and interview rooms, and all the intermediate floors down to the dungeons in the basement under, were rotten, and in some areas had completely collapsed. The death chamber at the south-east corner of this wing had the roof and floors in a very dangerous condition.

Coming back again to the central compound, which replaced an inner court surrounded by cells on four sides, was considered, when it was built in the 1850s, a classic of prison architecture. However, it was anything but a classic when we took it over in May of that year. The section of the roof which was glazed was almost devoid of glass, and what remained had persisted as a menace to the labour task force. In some places the steel glazing bars and the top weathering strip at the apex roof had rusted away.

The slated section to the south side of the roof was gone beyond repair and trees were growing out of the roof space over the third tier of cells. To the north side of the roof the picture presented in May was a little better than the south side, although there was a nice green sward of grass along the gutters and growing up the roof for about four feet.

Practically all cells in the central compound had the plaster hanging off the walls and ceiling. The galleries and the stairs leading thereto were rotten, although the basic structure of these galleries and stairs which is cast-iron remained substantially sound.

The stone floor to the central compound was ringed with bird droppings to a depth of 10 to 12", while young chestnut trees and luxurious ferns sprung from the joints in the stone floor and steps leading to the galleries. The kitchen, stores and punishment cells in the basement of the central compound were still sound and dry, but as elsewhere, all doors, windows, plumbing fixtures, etc., were missing. The laundry and drying rooms in the basement under the south wing of the '98 section were structurally sound and dry. The water and gas services to the jail had been disconnected many years ago, but the foul water drainage system was still connected to the main sewer.

What I have said is a thumbnail sketch of the condition of the buildings and yards in May 1960, and much to the dismay of the pigeons overhead and rats underfoot we set out to first push back the advance of nature and arrest the ravages of time and neglect.

After this visit I felt that the plans I had made for the restoration work were adequate both in regards to costs, labour content, and time, and all that now remained to be done was to submit the plans officially to the Minister for Finance, together with the names of our supporters. At this stage it should be mentioned that the finances for renting rooms, postage, etc., was provided by me and all the typing and duplicating was carried out by my office. Eventually Joe Groome provided us with the use of his sitting-room anytime we required it and this generosity to the project was maintained in different forms up to my departure from Kilmainham.

Seamus Bruce (third from left) with Kilmainham guides Rosemary Carder, Peter MacMahon and Mícheál Ó Doibhilín, when visiting the jail in June 2006.

APPENDIX 8

SEAMUS BRUCE, FORMER VOLUNTARY WORKER AT KILMAINHAM IN THE 1960S, INTERVIEWED IN JUNE 2006

I met Seamus Bruce one day when he came into the jail to do a radio interview speaking about the restoration. When he was finished I managed to speak with him for a few minutes and he agreed to talk to me. We arranged to meet later and I spent the intervening days trying to put together a list of questions for him. I might as well not have bothered, however, as Seamus was willing to talk about the restoration of the jail and those who worked on it – but at his own pace.

He told me that a management committee was set up in 1959 to lease the building from the government. Two of the negotiators were James (Seamus) Brennan and Mr Stevenson. Also on the committee was Piaras Mac Lochlainn, a civil servant, and Seamus referred to him as the 'brains' behind the 1966 exhibition, collecting the historical documents. Seán Dowling was chairman. Lorcan Leonard, a very patriotic man who made an enormous contribution to the restoration of the jail was the driving force behind the work.

A carpenter by trade, Seamus Bruce arrived at the site in May 1960, an employee of Dublin Corporation. He was living in Drimnagh at the time. Paddy Kelly and Charlie Gorman approached him and asked if he would like to be involved in the restoration of the building. Money was in short supply for restoration projects, so the jail was in danger of being demolished. The yards had between 40 and 50 trees and up to 1,000 saplings growing in them. Most of the yards were covered in brambles and slash hooks had to be used to cut a path through them. The glass and bars were missing in the windows and very little of the guttering remained. The roof lights were missing from the east wing. It took months to clear the rubbish from the building and it was dumped behind the infirmary. The outer walls were covered with up to two feet of ivy.

Finally, they could see the task ahead of them. Seamus felt that beneath the decay there was a great history to be told, on what he called sacred ground. A site committee was set to report to the management committee on the progress of the work. Lots of men and women volunteered to help but some were deemed unsuitable due to lack of qualifications. Some gave up their summer holidays and spare time to work on the project. Seamus felt that it was the duty of every Irishman to work on this project and, in that way, to give something back to his country.

As the work progressed, a guide committee was set up to give tours of the east wing and the yards. The cost of admission? Just a shilling!

Seamus was in charge of the restoration of the east wing, and he knew the task ahead was a daunting one. He designed the scaffolding so work could commence. The glass roof had fallen in and lay on the flagstones beneath, with six inches of pigeon droppings on top of it. The floor, stairs and metal work of the east wing were restored to their original condition, and the timber work replaced with wood from State forests.

Eleven thousand blue roof slates were used in re-roofing the jail, held in place by copper nails. Seamus worked on the project for ten years during his summer holidays. Surprisingly, no major accidents occurred while the men worked on the roof, all the more noteworthy as the winter of 1962 was the coldest the country had seen in one hundred years. Paddy Early was put in charge of roofing the west wing, while John Salmon restored the governor's quarters. Joe McGrath from the Irish Sweepstakes (himself a prisoner in Kilmainham Jail during the War of Independence) donated £1,000 per annum to help buy much-needed supplies, a very welcome and significant donation.

Young volunteers were receiving valuable training from the craftsmen on the site and many later gained employment in those areas in which they had worked. Romance always blossoms no matter where you go and the restoration of Kilmainham was no different. Seamus, for example, met his future wife, Philomena, as she helped out in the canteen.

Donations were coming in from all quarters. Toddy O'Sullivan, manager of the Gresham, sent up crates of beer and wine for the annual party for the workers. On one occasion, John Hanratty from the management committee asked de Valera why money was not provided by the government for the project, and he replied that he regretted it but that there just was not the money available in the country at the time.

On behalf of myself and the staff of the jail I would sincerely like to thank Seamus and his comrades for the great work that so selflessly was given by them, so Ireland and the Irish can continue to honour their history.

(*Source*: Article by Peter MacMahon in *Sentence*, June 2006.)

APPENDIX 9

KILMAINHAM JAIL
CONFRONTING CHANGE

Pat Cooke, Curator of Kilmainham Jail (1986-2007), explains how the jail's gradual metamorphosis from a place of exclusive nationalist reverence to one of increasing inclusivity was assisted by artistic interventions.

If it weren't for the monarchist associations, it would be tempting to describe Kilmainham Jail as one of the jewels in the crown of the OPW's portfolio of heritage properties. In any event, this disused jail has a good claim to be Ireland's most impressive national monument of the modern period, telling a story that is truly epic in its sweep. From the day it opened in 1796, to its closure in 1924 in the immediate aftermath of the Civil War, Kilmainham Jail seems to have registered each seismic shift in Ireland's struggle for, and eventual winning of, a measure of political independence from Britain. The list of prominent Irish political leaders of those years who were never in Kilmainham is a short one (O'Connell and Collins were among the few notables who escaped its grasp). But it seems that virtually everybody else was: most of the leading protagonists of the 1798, 1803, 1848, 1867 and 1916 rebellions; Republican prisoners of the War of Independence of 1919-21; and anti-Treaty prisoners during the Civil War of 1922-24. But its range of historical significance is not confined solely to the physical force tradition. Charles Stewart Parnell and virtually all of his Irish parliamentary party colleagues were prisoners in Kilmainham over the winter of 1881-82. Parnell effected his freedom by signing the so-called 'Kilmainham Treaty' with the British Prime Minister W.E. Gladstone, an agreement whereby the Irish Party promised to work with the Liberal Party to achieve Home Rule for Ireland, setting in train the political process that remained at the heart of Irish constitutional politics for the subsequent thirty years up to the outbreak of war in 1914.

Yet, while Kilmainham's prison records contain some of the star names of modern Irish history, it is not these alone that gives the jail's story its epic scale. As the county jail of Dublin, it was host not only to heroes, but to thousands of ordinary men, women and children, most of them Dubliners, and all of them affected by the social stresses and economic upheavals that governed their usually harsh lives. At the height of the Famine of the late 1840s, the place became overcrowded with the destitute and the starving. Many of them had deliberately committed petty offences in the hope that the meagre prison diet would save them. From the 1790s right through to the 1850s, it also served as the depot where prisoners sentenced to transportation from the east and north-east of Ireland were gathered together before being sent to Australia. Over 6,000 transportees passed through Kilmainham in these years, giving it a role in shaping the history not only of modern Ireland but Australia as well.

While this brief survey may give some sense of the richness and complexity of the site's history, it does nothing to convey the challenges involved in interpreting it for a broad-ranging contemporary audience, almost half of whom are foreign visitors.

For Kilmainham Jail remains a place of deeply contested meaning. For ardent republicans and nationalists, it will always be an authentic shrine of Irish patriotism. But for others it can raise some challenging questions. Throughout the years of the Northern troubles, the tenets of nationalist and republican faith were vigorously questioned by historians and intellectuals who no longer accepted its simple pieties. This revisionist debate has remained at the heart of Ireland's reassessment of national identity over recent decades, as we have struggled to come to terms with political violence in the North and the implications of a rapidly changing and increasingly secular society in the South.

In developing and interpretative strategy for Kilmainham Jail, therefore, one thing soon became clear enough: if our goal was to make the place an inclusive locus of historical exploration for people of all political persuasions, then ways would have to be found of placing it at the heart of this debate. This called for a delicate balancing act. On the one hand, the authenticity of the place as a locus of patriotic virtue, where men and women had suffered and died for their country, needed to be affirmed. But on the other, those questions about the validity and efficacy of the physical force tradition in the Irish struggle for political independence needed to be acknowledged, as did the jail's wider history as a place of incarceration for thousands of ordinary, unheroic people. This has not been an easy balancing act. Insofar as we have managed it, it has involved abiding clearly and consistently with two principles. First, the story of Kilmainham Jail as a place central to understanding the passions of Irish patriotism had to be told without apology or dilution. This is the essence of the guided tour of the jail, in which visitors are shown the cells where Emmet and Sarah Curran were held, the room where Parnell endured his privations, the yard where Padraig Pearse and thirteen of the leaders of the 1916 rebellion were shot by firing squad, and the place where four young republican prisoners were executed by Free State soldiers during the Civil War.

But what is the broader meaning and implication of these stories? To try to deal with this question we have pursued a second principle: a policy of cultural assess by *bona fide* artists. Since the site came into OPW care in 1986, we have facilitated artists and performers from a wide variety of backgrounds in making interventions that either overtly or subtly question the site's 'grand narrative'. A steady stream of artistic events, ranging from the visual arts, to theatrical and operatic performances, have been staged in the jail over the years. Earlier this year, Macedonian artist Elpida Hadji Vasileva created an exhibition based on visual parallels between the jail as a place of execution and execution sites in former Yugoslavia. Calypso Theatre Company will be staging a new play on the 1916 Rising by Donal O'Kelly as part of the 90th anniversary commemorations. And in September 2006, Opera Theatre Company (visitors on two previous occasions) will be returning to the east wing to stage Beethoven's *Fidelio* (which happens to be set in a prison).

One of the most significant events in this steady stream of art interventions was the 1991 exhibition 'In a State', a major art show in which twenty-one leading Irish artists from North and South, from Catholic and Protestant backgrounds, made works that responded directly to the history and symbolism of the jail. Not all of these interventions, it has to be said, have met with universal approval. In 2003, Canadian photographer Ron Levine staged an exhibition of his photographs entitled 'Prisoners of Age' in the east wing. His large-scale powerful images depicted the actual consequences of the throwing the key away once convicts end up in jail in some US states. They grow old and die there. But a lot of visitors (many of them American) had difficulties with this show. What has an exhibition about elderly prisoners in the jails of Alabama and Tennessee got to do with Irish history, they asked?

However, when you think about this question, you begin to see Kilmainham Jail for what it actually is — a disused jail. For virtually all of the world's jails share generic architectural roots in nineteenth-century notions of punishment. The east wing of Kilmainham, completed in 1856, is patterned off Pentonville Prison, itself the 'model prison' for virtually all other prisons built in these islands during the latter part of the nineteenth century. In this way, Kilmainham, as much as any other jail, becomes a platform for exploring issues of crime and punishment or more universal questions about bondage and freedom. The moment the site's potential for multi-layered meaning and symbolism is acknowledged, its capacity to become part of a genuinely post-colonial project is revealed, one in which its crystalline nationalist history can be simultaneously affirmed and transcended through a process of artistic exploration.

And would those who died here have had it different? Many of them were poets and artists themselves. For the visionaries among them, the winning of Irish independence would provide the freedom to achieve other kinds of freedom, connecting us in common humanity with unresolved issues of nationality and political freedom in the wider world. By combining orthodox historic site interpretation with artistic programming, Kilmainham Jail has become a heritage site that also works as a cultural space. The distilled message of these interventions is that the past is never quite another country; history is always an anxious ingredient in our contemporary consciousness.

Pat Cooke

(Originally published in *Obair*, Bulletin of the Office of Public Works, 2006)

ENDNOTES

[1] The jail is mostly referred to today in official literature by an older variation of the word – 'gaol'. This is as a result of a decision taken by the curator of the jail museum in the late 1980s in order to differentiate it from other functioning jails in Ireland. As the author takes as his subject the abandonment and eventual restoration of the jail as a national monument, he does not have to concern himself with such possible misunderstanding, and the modern variation of the word is used throughout.

[2] See Appendix 1.

[3] Peter Cassidy, James Fisher, John Gaffney and Richard Twohig were executed by firing squad in a yard of Kilmianham Jail on 17 November 1922.

[4] Éamon de Valera, Seán MacEntee, Seán T. O'Kelly, Tomás Derrig, Gerald Boland, Oscar Traynor, Frank Gallagher and many other members of the Fianna Fáil Party. Seán Lemass was held in nearby Richmond Barracks in 1916, as was James Ryan.

[5] The General Prisons Board had decided to close the jail in 1910 (the prisoners were transferred to Mountjoy Jail). Already in a deteriorating condition, the jail was used as an emergency detention barracks by the British army after the 1916 Rising and later during the War of Independence. The prison was used during and immediately after the Civil War by the Irish Free State army, to hold Republican prisoners. Numerous survivors' accounts of the 1916-24 period attest to the very poor condition of the jail.

[6] *The Irish Times*, 9 March 1927.

[7] Kilmainham Jail Closing Order, Kilmainham Jail Museum.

[8] Memorandum on Proposed Acquisition of Kilmainham Jail, Department of Finance, 30/8/1935, Department of the Taoiseach General Registered Files, S. 6521 AC.

[9] D. Fitzpatrick, 'Commemoration in the Irish free State' in I. McBride (ed.), *History and memory in Modern Ireland* (Cambridge, 2001), p.195.

[10] *Ibid.*, p.196.

[11] *Ibid.*

[12] *Ibid.*

[13] *Irish Independent*, 2 September 1931.

[14] The NGA was consciously following in the footsteps of earlier Fenian memorial committees. Two Fenians who had taken part in the rescue of Col. Kelly and Captain Deasy at Manchester in 1867 were among the founder members of the NGA in 1926.

[15] The NGA had unveiled a 1916 memorial in Glasnevin Cemetery and were regularly tending the graves of many Irish patriots throughout the country. In 1932, they produced an invaluable guidebook to the national graves and shrines in Dublin and district.

[16] See Appendix 2.

[17] The author was informed of another proposal that the jail might be used as a penitential hostel during the Congress, reflecting perhaps most particularly the chronic need for emergency accommodation at that time.

[18] Outlined in John Fitzpatrick's letter to Seán T. O'Kelly, 7/12/1932, National Graves Association file, Kilmainham Archives Collection.

[19] Letter from John Fitzpatrick to Seán T. O'Kelly, 7/12/1932, National Graves Association File, Kilmainham Archives Collection.

[20] Letter from O'Kelly to E. de Valera, 16/12/1932, Department of the Taoiseach Files, S. 6521 AC.

[21] Ibid.

[22] Letter from Secretary, Office of Public Works to Department of Taoiseach, 13/5/1936, Department of Taoiseach Files, S. 6521 AC

[23] Ibid.

[24] Ibid.

[25] Dáil Éireann, Volume 60, Column 968, 20/2/1936 – Kilmainham Jail.

[26] The Irish Amateur Boxing Association had made a request to the county council to be given a portion of the jail (obviously the large Victorian East wing) for conversion into a National Boxing Stadium. The council turned down the request.

[27] Wicklow People, 20 February 1936.

[28] The Irish Times, 17 December 1935.

[29] See plan of Jail in Appendix 4.

[30] Letter from Secretary, Executive Council to Secretary Department of Finance, 7/12/1936, Department of the Taoiseach Files, S. 6521 AC.

[31] The jail was acquired by the State in February 1937 for the nominal sum of £100 on the understanding that it would be developed as a national monument.

[32] The Irish Press, 14 March 1938.

[33] The Irish Press, 14 March 1938. To the fascination of later guides working in the jail, many of the former prisoners who visited on that day signed their names on the wall of the cell in which they were held.

[34] The jail had been opened to a number of groups before this by private arrangement. A commemoration ceremony was often included. This followed in an interesting tradition. The first commemoration ceremony in the jail was held by female republican prisoners in May 1923, honouring the 1916 leaders at their place of execution. Several of those female prisoners were directly related to the executed leaders.

[35] Ibid.

[36] The Irish Press, 20 March 1938.

[37] The Irish Times, 20 March 1938.

[38] A Seán Heuston memorial statue was unveiled in the park in 1943.

[39] Buckley also wrote an account of her experiences as a prisoner in Kilmainham, The Jangle of the Keys (1938).

[40] This open day was organised by the Easter Week Men's Association. De Valera was received by a guard of honour of 'Easter Week men'.

[41] The Royal Hospital Kilmainham and the Phoenix Park were considered as venues where the Dáil and Seanad could meet.

[42] This was first suggested by the Dublin Brigade Council of the Old IRA in 1935. A garden of remembrance would eventually be opened in 1966.

[43] Memo for the Government reviewing various plans for Kilmainham Jail, from Department of Finance, 17/5/1946, Department of the Taoiseach Files S. 6521 B.

[44] Department of the Taoiseach Files S. 6531 B.

[45] Memo for the Government from Department of Finance, 17/5/1946, Department of the Taoiseach Files, S. 6521 B.

[46] Government Meeting Note, Cabinet Item No.2, Kilmainham Jail, 13/7/1946, Department of the Taoiseach Files, S. 6521 B.

[47] Letter from Office of Public Works to Department of Defence, 30/10/47, Office of Public Works Files, A 41/7/2/37, OPW 9.

[48] Memo from the Commission of Public Works, 31/7/1953, reviewing various plans for the Jail, Department of the Taoiseach Files, S. 6521 C.

[49] *Ibid.*

[50] Dáil Éireann, Volume 101, Col. 453, 21/5/1946, Vote 9, Office of Public Works

[51] Letter from M. Quane to Dr Hayes McCoy (Officer in charge of Historical, etc., collections), 30/9/1953, Office of Public Works file, A 41/7/2/37, OPW 9.

[52] Letter from Department of Taoiseach to Department of Finance, 26/8/1953, Department of the Taoiseach Files, S. 6521 C.

[53] Press Release, 28/8/1953, Department of the Taoiseach Files, S. 6521 C.

[54] *The Irish Press*, 29 August 1953.

[55] Presumably a reference to Aer Lingus's purchase of a number of Constellation aircraft at this time.

[56] Dáil Éireann, Volume 149, Col. 115, 15 June, 1954, Resolution No.2, General.

[57] Dáil Éireann, Volume 146, Col. 1060, 1 July, 1954 – Kilmainham Jail.

[58] Letter from CPW to Department of Taoiseach, 15/10/1956, Department of the Taoiseach Files, S. 6521 D/63.

[59] A Shell garage was later erected on the site.

[60] Letter from Commissioners of Public Works to Department of Finance, 1 December 1955, NAI, DFA, S102/017/53.

[61] The garden of remembrance was finally opened in 1966. The particular site was chosen because the Irish Volunteers (Óglaigh na hÉireann) were founded there in 1913.

[62] *The Sunday Press*, 29 April 1958.

[63] *The Sunday Press*, 29 April 1958.

[64] Recollections of L. Leonard, no date, Restoration Files, Box 2, Kilmainham Archives Collection.

[65] *Ibid.*

[66] *Ibid.*

[67] A remarkable number of Old IRA members did indeed become members of the restoration committee.

[68] Department of the Taoiseach Note, 1/7/1958, Department of the Taoiseach Files, S. 6521 D/63.

[69] *Ibid.*

[70] *Ibid.*

[71] *Evening Herald*, 24 October 1958.

[72] Letter from James Brennan (Secretary of Old IRA Society) to Éamon de Valera, 27/10/1958, Department of the Taoiseach Files, S. 6521 D/63.

[73] Letter from Department of Finance to Department of Taoiseach, 30/10/1958, Department of Taoiseach Files, S. 6521 D/63.

[74] L. Leonard Recollections, no date, Restoration Files, Kilmainham Archives.

[75] See Appendix 3.

[76] The minister James Ryan was a 1916 veteran who had been in the GPO during the Rising.

[77] Letter from Department of Finance to Department of Taoiseach, 29/1/1960, Department of the Taoiseach Files, S. 6521 D/63.

[78] See Appendix 3.

[79] Memo for Government from Department of Finance, 13/2/1960, Department of the Taoiseach Files, S. 6521 D/63.

[80] Memo From Department of Education to Department of Finance, 26/2/1960, Department of Taoiseach Files, S 6521 D/63. See Appendix 4.

[81] See Appendix 3.

[82] The Irish Press, 30 April 1960.

[83] Dáil Éireann, Volume 181, No. 10, Col. 1371-2, 17/5/1960, Committee on Finance – Vote 8 – Office.

[84] See Appendix 5.

[85] The Irish Press, 28 May 1960.

[86] The infirmary building was badly damaged by fire in January 1962 but was soon restored once again.

[87] KJRS, Kilmainham Jail, The Bastille of Ireland, p.17.

[88] Kilmainham Archives Collection, L. Leonard Recollections.

[89] KJRS, Kilmainham Jail, The Bastille of Ireland, p.18.

[90] See Appendix 6.

[91] Kilmainham Jail Archives Collection, L. Leonard's Recollections.

[92] The Irish Press, 8 October 1960.

[93] Kilmainham Archives Collection, Restoration Files, Box 2.

[94] Ibid.

[95] The Irish Press, 18 March 1961.

[96] The Irish Press, 9 May 1961.

[97] Donations records, Restoration Files, Box 2, Kilmainham Archives Collection.

[98] Kilmainham Jail Museum, Restoration memorabilia.

[99] Newspaper cut-out, unnamed, undated, Restoration Scrapbook, Kilmainham Archives Collection.

[100] Messrs Cahill Printers provided 1,500 copies of the booklet free of charge.

[101] The Irish Press, 23 May 1961.

[102] Ibid.

[103] Department of Taoiseach note, 12/10/1963, Department of the Taoiseach Files, S. 6521 D/63.

[104] The Irish Press, 4 May 1964. Lemass was actually held in nearby Richmond Barracks after the Rising for one week.

[105] Letter from KJRS to Lord Killanin, 29/8/1963, Restoration Files, Box 2, Kilmainham Archives Collection.

[106] Restoration Files, Box 1, Kilmainham Archives Collection.

[107] President Kennedy did attend a 1916 commemoration ceremony at Arbour Hill and paid respect to the nationalist tradition in a number of his speeches in Ireland.

[108] Letter from Department of Finance to OPW, 23/2/1965, Department of the Taoiseach, Files S. 6521 D.

[109] Behan himself had special connections with the jail. He first saw his father from a high cell window on the east side of the jail in 1923 – his father being one of the republican prisoners held there at the time. Behan visited the jail in 1960 and offered his services as a painter but as he was apparently a little the worse for wear at the time his offer was politely refused. He visited again during the filming.

[110] Scenes for the screen adaptation of Frank O'Connor's *Guests of the Nation* were filmed in the jail in 1933.

[111] Lemass was particularly keen to have participation from voluntary national organisations, particularly the Old IRA Association, and many of the Kilmainham trustees and prominent voluntary workers were members of that organisation.

[112] *The Irish Press*, 11 April 1966.

[113] Department of External Affairs, *Cuimhneacháin 1916-1966* (Government Publications, 1966).

[114] *The Irish Press*, 11 April 1966.

[115] *Ibid.*

[116] RTÉ Guide, Easter 1966, Kilmainham Jail Museum.

[117] £117 from the first collection. There would be further collections from the pool.

[118] Important restoration work still had to be carried out in the older west wing of the jail but the east wing was the main priority.

[119] P.J. Stephenson died in 1959, before the restoration work had actually begun.

[120] *The Irish Times*, 16 June 1986.

[121] The KJRS continued to receive valuable and very interesting donations after 1966. Most spectacularly, Erskine Childers's yacht, the *Asgard*, was given on an extended loan to the society. The yacht, famous for the gun-running episode in 1914, was on public display in a yard of the jail from 1979-2002.

[122] The jail was then only open to the public for two hours on Sunday afternoons – even then it could be closed if filming was taking place.

[123] Previously referred to as the Commissioners of Public Works.

[124] P. Cooke, *A History of Kilmainham Gaol*, p.41.

[125] Some £25 million had been spent on the restoration of the Royal Hospital Kilmainham, which was completed in 1984. A National Centre for Culture and the Arts was established there in 1985. There was also a very considerable state investment in the restoration of the Custom House in Dublin in these years.

[126] Among many other examples, the jail also features in *The Italian Job*, *The Machintosh Man*, *The Last Remake of Beau Geste*, *The Old Curiousity Shop* and *The Escapist* (2008). Most fittingly, the 1984 film *Anne Devlin* documented the story of one of Kilmainham's famous prisoners.

[127] N. O'Sullivan, *Every dark hour, a history of Kilmainham Jail* (Dublin: Liberties Press, 2007), p.185.

[128] In association with the Irish Prison Education Service, a series of exhibitions of prisoners' art work have been displayed, from prisons throughout Ireland.

[129] Handel's *Tamerlane*, Beethoven's *Fidelio*, Shakespeare's *The Tempest* and Beckett's *Catastrophe* have also been performed at the jail. In 1923, female prisoners in Kilmainham staged Yeats's play *Kathleen ni Houlihan* in the east wing of the jail.

[130] With considerable detail now available on the 1916 executions in the jail, with the cells of virtually all of the 1916 leaders (and those of many other lesser known figures in the Rising) identifiable, with the wedding of one of the leaders, Joseph Plunkett, taking place in the chapel of the jail just hours before his execution, and with so many detailed accounts of the experiences in Kilmainham of these political prisoners, it is inevitable that the 1916 Rising is such a dominant feature of a tour of the jail.

[131] *The Irish Times*, 1 April 1991.

[132] The chairman of the Kilmainham Jail Restoration Committee, Seán Dowling, was even an artist, like Ballagh.

[133] A study carried out by Irish Marketing Survey on public attitudes to the Rising revealed that 65 per cent of respondents looked on the rebellion with pride, as opposed to a mere 14 per cent who said they regretted it. A further resounding 66 per cent felt that the 1916 leaders would oppose contemporary IRA violence.

[134] The final decommissioning of IRA weaponry took place in 2005.

[135] G. Doherty, 'The commemoration of the ninetieth anniversary of the Easter Rising' in G. Doherty & D. Keogh, '1916: the long revolution' (Cork: Mercier, 2007).

[136] He actually slept through that meeting, being only two years old.

[137] This included army, navy, Aer Corps, UN veterans, Gardaí, and support equipment/vehicles, and Aer Corps fly passes.

[138] There were 14,000 visitors in 1986 when the OPW took over the running of the jail.

[139] See Editorials of various national newspapers, 21-29 October 1966.

[140] Interview with Piarias McLoughlin, 1966 RTÉ Documentary on the Restoration, Kilmainham Jail Museum.

BIBLIOGRAPHY

PRIMARY SOURCES

National Archives:
Department of the Taoiseach General Registered Files, S. 6521, AC, B, C, D, D/63
Office of Public Works Files A 41/7/2/37, OPW 9

Kilmainham Archives Collection:
Restoration Files (miscellaneous)
Restoration Memorabilia

Newspapers:
Wicklow People
The Irish Times
Irish Independent
The Irish Press
The Sunday Press
Evening Herald

Dáil Éireann:
Various Dáil Debates, 1936–1960

SECONDARY SOURCES

Bew, Paul & Patterson, Henry, *Seán Lemass and the making of modern Ireland, 1945-66* (Dublin: Gill & Macmillan, 1982).
Bhreathnach-Lynch, Sighle, 'The Easter Rising 1916: constructing a canon in art and artefacts', *History Ireland*, Vol.v, No.1 (Spring 1997).

Boyce, D.G., '1916: Interpreting the Rising' in D.G. Boyce & A. O'Day (eds), *The making of modern Irish history: revisionism and the revisionist controversy* (London: Routledge, 1996).

Caulfield, Max, *The Easter rebellion* (London: Frederick Muller, 1964).

Carey, Tim, *Mountjoy: The Story of a Prison* (Cork: The Collins Press, 2000).

Coogan, Tim Pat, *De Valera, Long Fellow, Long Shadow* (London: Hutchinson, 1993).

Cooke, Pat, *A History of Kilmainham Gaol: 1796-1924* (Dublin: Government Publications, 1996).

Daly, Mary & O'Callaghan, Margaret, *1916 in 1966: Commemorating the Easter Rising* (Dublin: Royal Irish Academy, 2007).

Department of External Affairs, *Cuimhneachán 1916-1966, Commemoration: a record of Ireland's commemoration of the 1916 Rising* (Dublin: Stationery Office, 1966).

Doherty, Gabriel & Keogh, Dermot, *1916: The Long Revolution* (Cork: Mercier Press, 2007).

Dudley Edwards, Owen & Pyle, Fergus, *1916: The Easter Rising* (London: Macgibbon & Kee, 1968).

Edwards, Ruth Dudley, *Patrick Pearse: The Triumph of Failure* (London: Victor Gollancz Ltd, 1977).

Fitzpatrick, David, 'Commemoration in the Irish Free State' in I. McBride (ed.), *History and Memory in Modern Ireland* (Cambridge: Cambridge University Press, 2001).

Foster, R.F., 'History and the Irish question', in Brady, Conor (ed.), *Interpreting Irish history: the debate on historical revisionism 1938-1994* (Dublin: IAP, 1994).

Gallagher, Frank, *Days of Fear: A Diary of Hunger Strike* (Cork: Mercier Press, 1967).

Greaves, C. Desmond, *The Life and Times of James Connolly* (London: Lawrence & Wishart, 1961).

Kelly, Freida, *A History Of Kilmainham Gaol: The Dismal House Of Little Ease* (Cork: Mercier Press, 1988).

Kilmainham Jail Restoration Society, *The Bastille of Ireland* (Dublin, 1961).

Kilmainham Jail Restoration Society, *The Ghosts of Kilmainham* (Dublin, 1963).

Keogh, Dermot, *Twentieth Century Ireland: Nation and State* (Dublin: Gill & Macmillan, 1994).

Longford, Earl of & O'Neill, T.P., *Éamon De Valera* (Dublin: Gill & Macmillan, 1970).

Lee, J.J., *Ireland 1912-1985: Politcs And Society* (Cambridge: Cambridge University Press, 1989).

Martin, F.X., *The Easter Rising, 1916 and University College Dublin* (Dublin: Browne & Nolan, 1966).

Martin, F.X., '1916: myth, fact and mystery' in *Studia Hibernica*, No.7 (1967).

McCoole, Sinead, *Guns and Chiffon, Women Revolutionaries and Kilmainham Jail, 1916-23* (Dublin: Government Publications, 1996).

MacEoin, Uinseánn, *Survivors* (Dublin: Argenta Publications, 1980).

MacEoin, Uinseánn, *The IRA in the Twilight Years: 1923-1948* (Dublin: Argenta Publications, 1997).

O'Donnell, Peadar, *The Gates Flew Open* (Cork: Mercier Press, 1965).

O'Malley, Cormac, *Prisoners: The Civil War Letters of Ernie O'Malley* (Dublin: Poolbeg Press, 1991).

O'Malley, Ernie, *The Singing Flame* (Dublin: Anvil Books, 1978).

O'Sullivan, Niamh, *Every dark hour, a history of Kilmainham Jail* (Dublin, 2008).